Other Books by Barbara Moon

LIVING LESSONS

ON

INTIMACY WITH

CHRIST

By Barbara Moon

"Except where otherwise noted, Scripture quotations are taken from the
New American Standard Bible®,
Copyright © 1960, 1962, 1963, 1968, 1971, 1972, 1973,
1975, 1977, 1995 by The Lockman Foundation
Used by permission." (www.Lockman.org)

Verses marked KJV are taken from the King James Version

Illustrations © 2013 Jessica Ellen May

© 2013 Barbara Moon

TABLE OF CONTENTS

THANKS

To Debbie Sellmann, who encouraged me, suggested changes and whose numerous contributions made this devotional so much better. I appreciate all the work you did in spite of the hard times you were going through.

To Jess Ellen May, for her beautiful illustrations. It has been one of my dreams to have someone draw illustrations for me.

To Mary Hermann, for the idea to take some of my blogs and turn them into a devotional book.

Thanks, also, to Amy Moon, who checked out some chapters, and Sarah Shedd, who gave great input and screened for typos.

And to Bob Moon—I can't publish any book without you. I'm so grateful for your expertise and help.

INTRODUCTION

If you are reading this devotional book, then like me, you desire a strong, deep, intimate relationship with God. When I was young, I asked God to show me how to fulfill that desire. He was faithful to do so, though I found it easy sometimes and not so easy at other times. Along the way, I had some great teachers who explained verses and principles from the Bible in ways that helped me learn how to turn to Him when times are good, when it seems like everything is falling apart and every circumstance in between. These teachers are a huge part of my journey and I will quote them often. I hope their words will live on through mine.

As what I was learning became experience, whenever I talked with people searching for "more" with God, or with hurting people who desperately needed God's loving comfort and healing, intimacy with Him was the only answer I could give that has truly made a difference. I could only pass on to others what I knew would get them where they wanted to go. Because of some circumstances in my journey, I would not be here today if I had not found Jesus to be more real than the things I could see and touch. We *can* experience His presence, a closeness which He desires and for which He designed us.

Many of the circumstances the Lord has taken me through have involved struggles and emotional pain. Struggles, trials and hurts can take us down one of two paths: either the path of escape and bitterness or the path toward intimacy with Christ. When I learned how to deal with emotional pain and hold on to the Lord, I learned not to fear pain; but most of all what I learned brought deeper intimacy with Him. Webster tells us that intimacy is "the state of being closely acquainted" or "very familiar with someone." Intimacy has been given other connotations through the years, but its true meaning has to do with knowing and being known in a wonderful, glorious, deeply belonging manner.

In this book, I invite you to consider these topics that will help you find intimacy with Christ. I have purposely made each separate devotion within a chapter short so that you can take time to think about each one before going on to the next. I pray that you will find truth that sets you free and God's comfort that turns mourning into joy. Jesus Himself is the Joy we find in our living lessons.

Barbara Moon

My child, I made you; I want you to know Me as your love, your joy and your peace. I live in you and want to live through you. You are in Me. I long to comfort your hurts, heal your wounds and remove your fears. I love you beyond what you can imagine. Trust Me; seek Me; find me; know Me.

FAITH—THE FOUNDATION OF INTIMACY

"Faith is the substance of things hoped for, the evidence of things not seen." Hebrews 11:1

What is faith? Why does it matter? What makes it so important? Those seeking intimacy need answers to these questions. Faith is the basic foundation of all that happens in the Christian life—even salvation; therefore, it seems like a great place to begin, because when we hear or read truth, it *must be believed in order to change our lives*. Learning how faith works is an important path to intimacy.

This verse in Hebrews gives us a good definition. We may think of faith as something invisible and intangible, but according to Hebrews, faith is tangible and evident. Often we read this verse and think that faith is something that might be true, or might happen, if we hope enough. It's also common to think that the outcome of something we want to believe is dependent on some kind of performance such as prayer (talking to God) or good behavior. We feel that we must pray enough or use the correct words. But this verse says that faith is substance, something tangible. It is something we can count on. Something we can trust.

If the Bible says that faith is somehow tangible then it occurred to me one day that I must be looking at it from the wrong perspective. So I turned faith around in my mind and asked myself, what is it that I'm trusting in, what is the object of my faith? I realized that without an object of faith there would be no faith. If I'm going to sit in a chair, I believe the chair will hold me up. If I go out to start my car, I believe the car is going to start. If I want to get saved from my sin, I believe Jesus is going to save me.

In each of these examples about the *object* of my faith, I can see two things that are important about each one: 1) How reliable is it? 2) How well do I know it?

If I'm going to sit down in a chair, it better be a chair with four strong legs and a stable seat. I cannot just go by appearances—the legs might look strong but really be loose and ready to break. But if that chair is in my home or I know the owner, I most likely will not think too much about sitting down.

We operate chair faith almost without thinking. But trusting God can be another matter for most of us. We feel that we need a large amount of faith in order to trust God. And if that's true, the question arises, "Do I have enough, and if not, how do I get more of it?"

> ***Application:*** Do you wonder if you have enough faith? Is it frightening to think about trusting God? Do you fear what might He ask of you, or take from you? As you get to know Him, it will become easier to rely on Him.

"Without faith it is impossible to please Him." Hebrews 11:6a

If, as this verse says, it's impossible to please God without faith, we surely want to understand it. The problem is, we often look inside and find fear and doubt instead of faith. Many people want to have more faith and trust God, but deep inside they have an unconscious fear of His reliability. This fear brings more real questions such as, "Will He do what He says?" "Will He take care of my problems, meet my needs and heal my wounds?" "How can I know He is reliable enough to place my life into His hands?" "How can I increase my faith?" I love an old story that answered these questions for me. The story is from a Texas pastor, Ron Dunn, who has since gone to be with Jesus. It went something like this:

> *I went to northern Michigan to do a conference. A friend wanted to drive me out to a nearby lake. As we drove along the lake, I noticed fishermen, sitting on the ice, out in the middle of the*

lake. They had cut holes in the ice and had dropped their lines into the water below. Since I am from the Southwest, I could not imagine sitting on ice to fish. Suddenly my friend turned toward the lake and told me he was going to drive out on it. I panicked. How could anyone drive a car out onto the lake? I was not about to go out on the lake in a car. I did not even want to walk out on the ice. When I nervously questioned my friend as to how all these people could drive a car onto the lake, he quickly answered, "They know the ice."

And there Pastor Dunn answers our list of questions about faith—***We desire to trust Him and know He is reliable by getting to know Him, the object of our faith.***

If we want to know that God is reliable we can do so by getting to know who God is and what He is *really* like, not what we *feel* He is like or what others have *told* us He is like. There are many mistaken views of God out there. Let's look at some ways that help us know Him better:

One of the first ways I got to know God better was by reading the Psalms over and over. In them I could see God's character. I did not focus on what some teachers call "the wrath of God," but rather focused on all the places the Psalms talk about His loving kindness, His mercy, His provision, His power. As I studied the New Testament, I saw His grace and love poured out through the Lord Jesus. We can know Him by knowing and believing what the Scriptures say about Him.

> *Application:* Do you have a habit of reading the Bible? The Psalms are a good place to start. You can read five Psalms a day and in one month you will have read all 150 of them. Read one Proverb a day and in one month you will have read them all. The Book of John is a good New Testament place to begin.

"I will say to the LORD, 'My refuge and my fortress, My God in whom I trust." Psalm 91:2

Remember the story about the ice fishermen in Michigan from the previous devotion? Learning to talk to God is another way He has used to "prove the ice" to me. In order to know Him and His voice better, I listened to people who already knew Him and who trusted Him. In the early years, most of the people that were helping me were on cassette tapes, the mp3's of my time. I wore them out listening over and over. I got to know God the same way we get to know anyone else—by spending time with Him and His friends who knew more than I. Peter Lord, a pastor in Florida, told us to "look at God's face instead of His hand," to love Him for who He is not for what He does. We will look more at this concept in the chapter on "Prayer and Communion."

As I grew in knowing God, I found it easier to step out and take some risks to see if God really was reliable. I love the scene in *Indiana Jones, The Last Crusade*, where Indy is about to cross the chasm to find the chalice. He has made it through dangerous obstacles; he has his notes and clues. He looks fearfully at the deep canyon below as he ponders those clues. At last, he steps out by faith into the void and his foot hits a rock bridge. Now his perspective changes and he can see the hidden bridge that is completely reliable to hold him up. Like Indiana Jones, as I began "proving" God's reliability, I walked to the edge of all the light I had—and took one more step. I'm sure that Indiana Jones felt as scared and crazy as we do when we first step out from the places we can see and touch and explain, past the edge of light we have, taking one more step and relying completely on the unseen and unexplainable.

We cannot take that one more step without in some way knowing and depending on the *object* of our faith to be there with that first step into the unknown. That dependence only needs to be the size of a mustard seed (extremely small) in order to take that first step. As I learned to trust Him and stepped out with some baby steps, God kept His word and I found Him to be absolutely reliable.

Having faith the size of a small seed and stepping out into the unknown remind me of when our young family joined Campus Crusade for Christ staff (now called Cru). We had no idea what we were getting ourselves into to leave a secure, fairly well-paying job to join a faith ministry. We would only get a paycheck if faithful, loving people sent donations to our account with Crusade. For the next twenty years, we lived by this kind of faith for finances, changing ministries two more times and rearing four children to adulthood relying on God's faithfulness. He did not fail—ever—not once.[1]

Each new step of faith I took to believe God showed me how the people fishing and driving on the ice in northern Michigan could trust it to

---

[1] For more on His faithfulness financially, see my book *Jesus Never Fails, Stories of God's Faithfulness,* www.lulu.com/barbaramoon

hold them–they knew the ice–how thick and strong it was. And like those who drive their cars onto the frozen lake, the more I knew God, the more I trusted Him. In the same way you would not trust a stranger to take your child for ice cream, it's difficult to trust God if you don't know Him. But you will trust a close friend with your child. Each little step I took that proved His faithfulness built my understanding of who He is. It became easier to trust Him and see how "faith is assurance and evidence" because I kept growing in how well I knew the One who is asking for my trust.

When one takes that first step of faith and finds the object of faith (God) there and dependable in the small steps, then God will take those baby steps that we make and grow our dependence with greater steps of faith. Salvation, believing that Jesus will save me if I ask Him to, may be our first step of faith, but the rest of our lives, as we have seen from the verses above, we will take other first steps in different areas. I saw that happen as I grew in knowing God and understanding more about myself. He has walked me through bigger and more difficult places to step out and believe Him in spite of the material evidence. Eventually I came to understand that Faith is a Person, Jesus Himself. I didn't really need "more" faith, I just needed to know Him who is my faith. Faith is tangible because He lives in me, He is reliable and I know He keeps His word. I've settled my definition of faith to be something like this: "Faith is saying and acting on whatever God says about something—and *whatever means whatever*."

Application: When, like Indiana Jones or the ice fishermen, you find yourself needing to trust God—be brave, take a chance, step out into what may feel unknown and frightening. Learn His voice and what He is like. I know you will find Him faithful.

"The righteous shall live by faith." Habakkuk 2:4

Growing in faith has its ups and downs. While serving with Campus Crusade for Christ when our children were young, we had ample opportunities to test the "ice." Finances were slim and the only money we received was through donations. While living in Washington, D. C. our oldest son, Jim, needed braces. By faith, not knowing how we would pay for braces, we took him to an orthodontist. After the consultation, the dentist said he would do the braces for half price. That was great. But when that oldest also needed dermatology care, we waited too long to take him by faith and see what God would do. Scars were the price he paid for our unbelief that time.

After living in D. C. for almost three years, our time with Campus Crusade came to an end. We moved to a suburb of Atlanta to serve with another Christian ministry. A lesson I was learning from the teachers to whom I was listening at that time was this: "God has the supply before we have the need—if I don't get it, I didn't need it." Shortly after moving, three days went by without milk for four growing children. I was not a happy mother. But if I believed what I was hearing and was going to practice it, I had to say by faith, "Milk every day is not a need." It was not easy to say because I'd always thought that milk was an every-day need.

In my struggle to believe God would provide food when it wasn't always visible, I did not always walk by faith. I cut corners by being very careful with food, even to the point of rationing. Slowly God taught me to look at Him and not the lack of finances. This took a very long time and I quite often fretted and complained. But deep in my heart I wanted to have to trust God like this. I truly wanted to know Him as Provider instead of just saying the words, "God provides." Exercising faith was the path to experience God as more than just words.

As we trusted God for financial needs, I believe it was also good for our children not to have everything they wanted or all that their friends had. They learned to pray for some of the special things they wanted, like Izod shirts and Guess jeans. One Christmas season after our third son, Greg, said he wanted an Izod, we told him to ask Jesus for it. On Christmas day, he received three Izod shirts for which we had not paid. He saw that God even provides special things sometimes. When old enough, the children learned to work for money, doing part time jobs. They learned to be dependable and how to do a good job, how to work well. They learned to spend well (most of the time) and save.[2]

The years of ups and downs, struggling to trust—and failing at times—were part of the journey, but even the struggles served to prove God's love and faithfulness. I had opportunity to grow in grace and intimacy when I had to stand on His words that He would provide even when it seemed He didn't come through until the stroke of midnight. Failures were an opportunity to grow in intimacy with Him by not taking self-condemnation and by keeping my eyes on His face.

> ***Application:*** Are you struggling financially and not certain that God will meet your needs? Keep believing and getting back up when you fail. Try asking God for something small and tangible so that when you receive it you will be able to say with assurance, "God answered this prayer for a need I had."

"For thus says the LORD God of Israel, 'The bowl of flour shall not be exhausted, nor shall the jar of oil be empty, until the day that the LORD sends rain on the face of the earth." I Kings 17: 14.

"Faithful is He who calls you, and He also will bring it to pass." I Thessalonians 5: 24

---

[2] To read how trusting God for finances affected the children, see their adult stories in *Jesus Never Fails, Stories of God's Faithfulness,* www.lulu.com/barbaramoon pages 80-86

In I Kings 17 we meet the prophet, Elijah, who declared to King Ahab that there would be no dew or rain on Israel for three years because the people were worshipping idols and Ahab had married a pagan woman. For a while, God provided food for Elijah beside a brook which eventually dried up. The Lord then sent Elijah to stay with a Gentile widow until the drought was over, working miracles for them to have food. God proved His faithfulness to Elijah and saved the widow from starvation as she trusted Elijah and his God.

Joining a faith ministry with four young children felt about as scary as I imagine it felt to live through three years without rain. Deciding to live by faith was a huge step for our family, but it brought many opportunities to see God's faithfulness as He taught us to trust Him. During the time for raising support we saw many "miracles." There were times that I felt like God was stretching our peanut butter and jelly supply just as He did the flour and oil for Elijah and the widow. Money appeared in our mailbox in brown paper bags, unsolicited checks and invites to dinner got us through to the next payday; friends repaired broken cars and broken irons.

Jim, our growing twelve year-old outgrew his Sunday shoes in one week. The kids and I prayed for God to provide new shoes for him. On Wednesday after returning home from church, I found $20 in my purse. The new shoes cost $20.

Greg, our nine year old, chipped his front tooth. While sharing about our work at a friend's house, a young man we didn't know volunteered to fix the tooth. He was a dentist. He gave all six of us free check-ups.[3]

These are just a few examples of how God built my faith when our family first began trusting Him for our financial needs. As I prayed for specific needs that arose, I learned how faithful God is and also how creative. Finding money in my purse, and in the mailbox, was fun and touching as I watched God use many different people along the way.

Application: If you find yourself out of a job or have changes in your income, I can tell you that you can trust God to provide. You may

---

[3] Stories from *Jesus Never Fails*, by Barbara Moon, www.lulu.com/barbaramoon

be very scared, but take the risk to pray and wait and see how His faithfulness will show up in your circumstances.

"And God is able to make all grace abound to you, always having all sufficiency in everything, that you may have an abundance for every good work." II Corinthians 9:8

Living by faith financially did not always *feel* like we had all sufficiency in everything, but God made His grace abound in spite of our feelings and doubts. Garage sales, friends handing me $100 for Christmas presents, and invitations to dinner all helped us through the early days with little income.

Enough financial support was finally raised and we were sent to Orlando, Florida, for training. There we lived in an apartment complex with other staff people. One Sunday, our family and another family drove over to Titusville to hear Rev. Peter Lord, one of the pastors I listened to on cassette tapes. There were eleven of us in our van. After the service ended, we went out to the van and discovered that it would not start. We were almost two hours from home with seven young children. Across the parking lot, a man heard us cranking the engine over and over. He walked up to my husband, Jim, studied the van for a moment then said, "I think your timing belt is broken." As they talked, the man realized we were from Orlando, looked at all the children standing around, plus the four adults, and offered his own van for us to drive home. We were shocked! A stranger was giving us his van to drive, going to have ours towed to a shop, and we could keep his as long as it took for the repairs? Unbelievable! "All sufficiency" was provided by a loving Heavenly Father and one of His children who lived what he heard preached! We became friends with this wonderful man and his wife.

When we finished training in Florida, the day finally arrived for us to go to our first assignment. We were surprised and scared to be told that we would be moving to the Washington, D.C. area. The cost of living there was far higher than any place we had ever lived. How would we pay rent or ever be able to buy a house? As we prepared to move, one evening at church there was a speaker who had survived a terrible plane crash with burns over much of his upper body and face. The man had come to know Jesus after the accident and he had a moving testimony. We invited him and his wife to go home with us and over the next week or so, as we shared about our move to D. C., Jerry offered to give us $10,000 to buy a house. Jerry's gift was a remarkable example of "an abundance for every good work!"

The blessings continued after buying the best house in Northern Virginia we could find for our $10,000 down payment. Other friends not only gave us $2,000 to make a bedroom in the basement, they drove to Virginia from Tennessee to do the remodel. Now our oldest child would have his own room again.

God's sufficiency abounded all through the years that we lived by faith for our financial provisions as He provided money for the children to do chorus trips and sports. We attended conferences in many states and traveled for training. We moved from Virginia to Georgia, upgrading our house because the cost of living was lower. Friends replaced broken appliances and roofed that house. The struggles were sometimes difficult and my faith wavered now and then, but through it all I learned that God keeps His word and that He is faithful and trustworthy.[4]

Application: When you feel needy, remember that God keeps all of His promises. He cannot lie. Abundance can come in many disguises, not just money, so look around for other blessings that He is pouring out on you. He does not promise to make you rich financially; He promises to always be with you, to provide for your needs, and He promises an abundant life—life to the full.

---

[4] Finance stories from my stories of God's faithfulness in *Jesus Never Fails; www.lulu.com/barbaramoon*

"Faith is the substance of things hoped for, the evidence of things not seen." Hebrews 11:1

I trust you have found some help with answers to your questions about faith and God and that you will find it easier to trust Him. He is worthy of your trust and worth getting to know. Faith as a way of life will bring substance to your life as you claim God's promises even when it feels like they could not possibly be true. I assure you that He is reliable and whatever it takes to find intimacy with Christ is worth the effort.

SALVATION—THE FIRST STEP TO INTIMACY

GOD GAVE HIS ONLY SON

"For God so loved the world that He gave His only begotten Son, that whoever believes in Him should not perish but have eternal life." John 3:16

As we are getting to know God, along the way we'll make many discoveries about Him. We will likely do things to test His trustworthiness. It will be easy to compare Him to our earthly relationships. We'll wonder if He truly loves *us personally*, not just the world. Beginning a relationship with God through His Son, Jesus Christ, will set us on the road to these discoveries. Exploring all that Jesus did for us and what it means for us who know Him is like going on a treasure hunt to find a chest filled with gold and jewels. The explorations, promises and rewards are endless. When we realize what God did through Jesus, we will begin to know that He loves us more than we can ever know. He made us relational beings and wants us to know intimacy with Him. Jesus makes it possible.

When God sent His Son to die for us, He did all that's necessary for us to know Him and His great love. Perhaps you can imagine how you as a parent could give your life to save your own child, but to give a son's life, or ask a son to give his life, is much more difficult to imagine. Why would God give His Son's life for us? How was such a thing possible? It was easier to understand these questions when I heard this story by Don Richardson, a missionary back in the '60's, to the Sawi tribe in New Guinea.

The Sawi people were a vicious tribe who plotted to betray other tribes and kill their people. As Mr. Richardson struggled to find a way to help the Sawi tribe understand the Gospel, he discovered that when two warring tribes wished to make real peace, they gave their baby son to the other tribe. The child was called a "peace child." Mr. Richardson drew the parallel with God's gift of His Son and they got the picture. They understood the value God placed on us when He sent Jesus because they knew how difficult it was to give their son to a former enemy.[5]

Like the Sawi people, our first step to intimacy with Christ is to receive Him as Savior and Lord. God's love is far greater than any earthly love; it is unfathomable. We can trust the God who loves us so much that He gave His only Son so that we might know Him and have eternal life. That is how much He loves you and me.

WE ARE SEPARATED FROM GOD BY OUR SIN

"All have sinned and come short of the glory of God." Romans 3:23

"For the wages of sin is death, but the free gift of God is eternal life in Christ Jesus our Lord." Romans 6:23

What makes a man be willing to take his family to the other side of the world to live among dangerous people who eat each other? Don Richardson and many others like him know this: "all have sinned and come short of the glory of God," and the result is death. When we understand the consequences of sin and coming short of God's glory, we long to help others find their way to God. The "wages of sin" is a death that is far worse than dying physically—it is spiritual death that separates us from God forever. In the Garden of Eden, God told Adam and Eve not to eat the

---

[5] *Peace Child*, Don Richardson, Regal Books, Ventura, CA, 2005, www.peacechild.org

forbidden fruit or they would "surely die." (Genesis 3:17) They ate the fruit, but they did not die physically right there—they died spiritually—and their relationship with God changed from completely intimate to one of shame and hiding. They were now separated from God. All of their descendants would likewise be separated unless God did something to restore them.

Romans 6:23 tells us that because of sin we are spiritually dead and hopelessly separated from God and that God did do something to bring us back to life. Since being separated from God because of sin is a significant truth that we need to understand well, in the next chapter we will look more closely at the reason we all have sinned and come short of the glory of God, but for now, we will take God at His word here in Romans.

God knew that mankind was going to reject Him, but He wanted to be with us so much that He made us anyway, providing us a way back before creation. Revelation 13:8 KJV tells us that Jesus was "slain before the foundation of the world." God had His free gift ready.

JESUS HAS PAID THE PENALTY FOR OUR SIN

"For He delivered us from the domain of darkness and transferred us to the kingdom of His beloved Son, in whom we have redemption, the forgiveness of sins." Colossians 1:13-14.

God's free gift to the world is eternal life through Jesus—the opposite of separation. Jesus' death on the Cross and His resurrection make forgiveness, salvation, and then intimacy, possible. Paul gives us evidence of Christ's work on the Cross in this verse from Colossians. If we receive Christ, He moves us from darkness to life with Him. He had to die to pay the penalty for our sin.

All through the Scriptures, God has required a sacrifice of blood for forgiveness. Hebrews 9:22 says, "And according to the Law, one may almost say, all things are cleansed with blood, and without shedding of blood there is no forgiveness." Romans 5: 8-9 tells us, "But God demonstrates His own love toward us, in that while we were yet sinners, Christ died for us. Much more then, having now been justified by His blood, we shall be saved from the wrath of God through Him."

When we receive Christ we are forgiven, redeemed, reconciled and justified. He has done what was necessary for us to be found and saved. Jesus is the way to salvation and intimacy: "Jesus said to him, 'I am the way, the truth and the life. No one comes to the Father but through Me.'" John 14:6

Application: It may sound strange to you that a blood sacrifice is necessary for forgiveness, but this is what God says is necessary and Jesus was willing to shed His. Take some time to consider what Jesus went through to pay the penalty for your sin. Thank Him for what He did. If you have not received Him into your heart, how to do so will become clear as we continue.

GOD LOVES US AND WANTS US TO BE SAVED

"For the Son of Man has come to seek and to save those who are lost." Luke 19:10

Have you ever been lost or lost one of your children? I remember when my oldest son, Jim, was about seven. We were at the county fair and suddenly we turned around and he was not with us. My heart dropped to my knees. I felt like I was going to throw up. We did not even know where to start looking. Right about then, over the loudspeaker, we heard the call,

"Would the parents of Jimmy Moon please come to the security booth?" Those were the sweetest words I had ever heard. My boy was found and safe. A policeman had found him and taken him to security.

Like the joy I felt when I found my son, God feels even more joy than we do when He finds one of His lost children. All of Heaven rejoices when just one is found and saved. (Luke 15:10)

I remember another time when one of my other children was lost and I didn't even realize it. We were in Florida with our four children, visiting my sister and her family with four children. After evening church we all twelve piled into their station wagon and went to McDonald's. After eating, we piled back into the car without counting heads. We were back home putting on pajamas for bedtime when I realized Bobby, age 6, was not there. I could not believe it. We had left him at McDonald's. He didn't know any phone numbers and I was not sure he even knew his uncle's last name. My sister called the McDonald's as the Dads left to go back. Bobby had gone to the restroom when we left. He didn't panic, but went to the counter and told them he was left behind. Daddy found him in the manager's office waiting patiently. He had eight boxes of cookies to take home to the siblings and cousins.

God never forgets His children or loses them. He never leaves His children behind. He has made a way for His children to be with Him forever and that is what His heart longs for. But we have to receive the gift He is offering.

Application: Have you been found by God? Have you received His gift? If not, keep reading so you can be a child who is no longer lost.

WE MUST RECEIVE HIM

"For by grace are you saved through faith, and that not of yourselves, it is the gift of God, not as a result of works that no one should boast." Ephesians 2:8-9

"Jesus answered and said unto him, 'Truly, truly I say to you, unless one is born again he cannot see the kingdom of God.'"

God is holding out a gift to anyone who will receive that gift. It's a gift so profound that you are "born again." God did everything to make the gift possible. All it takes is for us to exercise faith to receive it. The gift is Christ Himself, a new life on Earth, eternal life with Him forever, and no separation from God. The gift is by His grace, not by anything that we can do to earn it.

All of us anticipate Christmas or birthdays, excited to see what gifts we will receive and what gifts we will give. Age does not matter; we all love gifts. In spite of the old song about "naughty" or "nice," we seldom buy a gift for a loved one based on how they have performed all year. We usually want to pick something that shows we care about them. This attitude in giving is grace. If we have a special gift for which we've hunted, debated and sacrificed to give someone, we would never decide to keep it in a closet.

Let's picture a little girl who has saved her money to buy a present for her cousin whom she will see at the family Christmas party. She goes to the party and smiles as she places her special present under the tree. One by one the presents are distributed until only her small gift lies alone under the tree—her cousin ignored the gift. It was bought for him, addressed to him and brought for him. But is the gift his? Not really. When does that gift belong to the loved recipient? Only after he receives it, after he takes it as his.

This is how we receive God's gift to us—we admit we need His gift; we believe He has done all that is necessary to get us the gift—and we accept His gift of salvation in the person of Jesus. We do not leave the gift under the tree.

> ***Application:*** Has God offered you His gift of eternal life with Jesus and you have left it un-acknowledged? If you have received the gift of Jesus, are there other "gifts and promises" from Him that you are not receiving, such as trusting Him when you are fearful or relying on Him to provide your needs? All of God's loving gifts are here for the taking by faith.

"If you confess with your mouth Jesus as Lord and believe in your heart that God raised Him from the Dead, you shall be saved." Romans 10:9

"But as many as received Him to them He gave the right to become children of God, even to those who believe in His name." John 1:12

"Behold I stand at the door and knock; if anyone hears My voice and opens the door, I will come into him and will dine with him and he with Me." Revelation 3:20

It's wonderful to hear and understand all that God has done for us through Christ, but it's even more wonderful to act upon what we've heard by faith. We don't have to understand all about it and we do not have to clean ourselves up in order to receive the right to become a child of God. We simply say with our mouth that we agree that Jesus is who He says He is and believe that He died for us and rose again. We admit we are a sinner and need Him to save us. We open the door to our heart and invite Him in. Jesus is a gentleman and waits to be invited. We *thank Him* that He has forgiven us, cleansed us and made us a child of God. As we grow in knowing what salvation is all about, the intimacy of "dining with Him" will become evident.

WE HAVE ASSURANCE OF SALVATION

"And the witness is this that God has given us eternal life, and this life is in His son. He who has the Son has the life; he who does not have the Son of God does not have the life. These things I have written to you who believe in the name of the Son of God, in order that you may know that you have eternal life." 1 John 5:11-13

Assurance of salvation is vital to growing as a Christian and experiencing intimacy. In these verses, John is showing us an easy way to know for certain. He simply says—if you have the Son, you have the life. Did you ask Jesus into your heart and receive the gift of salvation? If so, you have the Son—and the life.

Sometimes when children are growing up they wonder if they're adopted. It's not unusual for kids to wonder such things when they're being disciplined or they don't seem to look like others in their family. Wondering whether we belong or not can be very upsetting; it will affect how we live. If we feel like we don't belong, we might get angry easily; we live with doubts and fears about the future. In the same way, if we don't know that we are "for sure saved," we will live in fear that we might not go to Heaven. Worrying about our salvation can interfere with intimacy with Jesus because we are not certain He will be there for us. When bad things happen we might think it's punishment from God.

Once we receive Christ, or even if it's been a while and we have doubts, it helps to write it down somewhere, perhaps in our Bible, as if driving a stake into the ground. We can write something like this: "Today, (the date) I am "driving this stake" to say that I know I have received Christ as my Savior. Whenever I feel doubts, I will remember this date or look at this place."

When my daughter, Jodi, was about five years old, she asked us if she could ask Jesus into her heart. Daddy asked her if she had ever done anything wrong. She said with upward inflection, "Noo." So Daddy said they would talk about it later. A couple of years later Jodi asked again if she could ask Jesus into her heart. When Daddy asked if she had done anything wrong, she hung her head and said softly, "Yes." So Daddy led her in the prayer to receive Christ. The next week Jodi and I cross-stitched "I asked Jesus into my heart on _____." She hung it on her wall.

> ***Application:*** Settle within yourself that you have assurance of salvation—if not, nothing else in your journey with Christ will work.

WE HAVE ETERNAL SECURITY

"My sheep hear My voice and I know them, and they follow Me; and I give eternal life to them, and they shall never perish and no one shall snatch them out of my hand. My Father, who has given them to Me is greater than all and no one is able to snatch them out of the Father's hand." John 10:27-29

"Who shall separate us from the love of Christ? Shall tribulation, or distress, or persecution, or famine, or nakedness, or peril or sword?" . . . Romans 8: 35

"I am convinced that neither death nor life, nor angels, nor principalities, nor things present, nor things to come, nor powers, nor height, nor depth, nor any other created thing, shall be able to separate us from the love of God which is in Christ Jesus our Lord." Romans 8: 35, 38-39

"In Him, you also, after listening to the message of truth, the gospel of your salvation—having also believed, you were sealed in Him with the Holy Spirit of promise, who is given as a pledge of our inheritance. . ." Ephesians 1: 13-14

"He Himself has said, 'I will never leave you nor forsake you.'" Hebrews 13:5

It's my opinion that worrying about one's salvation, a controversial topic among denominations, is one of the worst fears in the world. I will not go into any controversies here because the next chapter explains what happens when we are born again, and that helps put the controversy to rest. (John 3:3) For now, I want us to look at these verses here, a representative few, in light of salvation being eternally secure. Read each one again.

Paul and John tell us that no one and no created thing (that includes us, ourselves) can take us away from our Heavenly Father. Jesus tells us that He will never go away.

Paul tells us in Ephesians 1:14 that the Holy Spirit is our pledge—our "earnest money" is the picture in the Greek. Just as we put down earnest money to buy a house, God promises to keep His word as we are sealed in Christ by the Holy Spirit.

At times it may be easy to judge someone's behavior and decide they are not a Christian based on what we can see. As observers we have to leave that question between them and God. I Samuel 16:7 tells us, ". . . for man looks at the outward appearance, but the LORD looks at the heart."

Forgetting about or feeling like the salvation experience did not happen can cause us to be concerned that we were not "really saved." We are usually basing that on behavior, also. It's very important that, if we doubt, we take time to make sure. At some point there comes a time to believe that salvation has come and then stand on the fact that it cannot be lost by anything we do. If we are certain we have received Christ, let us be assured that we cannot lose it regardless of behavior—or how we feel.

My third son, Greg is a good example of forgetting one's salvation experience, probably because he was so young. Greg was about five when he asked Jesus into his heart one day sitting at the little kids' table in our den. A few years went by and he told me one day that he was not sure he would go to Heaven when he died. He did not remember that day in the den. So we led him through the prayer again, marking it up to his young age. Then we wrote down in his Bible that he had asked Jesus into his heart that day. A year or so went by and one day as Greg and I were talking he said something like, ". . . you know, Mom. That day I asked Jesus into my heart sitting at the little table in the den back in Huntsville." For some reason he remembered the time when he was five. Either way, Greg is saved and secure.

My maiden name was "Ford." I was born a Ford and even if I tried to act like and look like the Smiths next door, I would still be a Ford. My behavior cannot change who I am. I changed my name after getting married, but in essence I am still a Ford. The only way I could be someone else is to die and be re-born. In the next chapter on Grace and Union we will look at how we get a new identity by dying with Christ to our old life and being reborn in Him.

Application: Do you know beyond a shadow of doubt that if you die tonight you will go to Heaven to be with Jesus? Do you know your salvation is secure regardless of behavior or feelings? Ponder these verses and trust God at His word that nothing you can do will take you out of His hand.

WE CAN EXPERIENCE VICTORY OVER SIN

"Who shall separate us from the love of Christ? Shall tribulation, or distress, or persecution, or famine, or nakedness, or peril or sword?" . . . In all these things we overwhelmingly conquer through Him who loved us. Romans 8: 35, 37

"But thanks be to God who gives us the victory through our Lord Jesus Christ." I Corinthians 15:57

"For whatever is born of God overcomes the world. And this is the victory that has overcome the world—our faith." I John 5: 4

Thanks be to God who always leads us in His triumph in Christ, and manifests through us the sweet aroma of the knowledge of Him every place." II Corinthians 2:14

These verses tell us that victory and triumph are part of our birthright in Christ. We will look at how this works out as we go through our next couple of chapters. Be ready to claim by faith that you are more than a conqueror. The picture here in the Corinthian's verse is like that of a soldier returning from battle in Jesus' day, dragging his conquered foe behind him, tied to his chariot. Through our salvation, we are conquerors because Jesus has defeated the enemy. As victorious and triumphant conquerors, we have intimacy with our Captain. That intimacy we have with Jesus is a sweet aroma to all those who meet us, drawing them to want to know Him as well.

Application: Do you know the sweet feel of victory because you rely on Jesus to bring you through your battles? Do you know the enemy is defeated and tied to His chariot? Ask Jesus to show you how you can be the "sweet aroma" to those around you.

WE MUST SURRENDER TO JESUS IN ORDER TO EXPERIENCE ALL HE HAS FOR US.

"I urge you therefore, brethren, by the mercies of God, to present your bodies a living and holy sacrifice, acceptable to God which is your spiritual service of worship. Do not be conformed to this world, but be transformed by the renewing of your mind, that you may prove what the will of God is, that which is good and acceptable and perfect." Romans 12:1-2

Total surrender is another controversial topic. The question arises whether a person can be saved or not without surrendering. Again, I will not go into the controversies as to when it should or does happen, but will look at the reasons it is important. Presenting ourselves as a "living sacrifice," means death to our selfish ways as we surrender to Jesus to have His way. It means that we will listen to, love, serve and obey God in all areas and ways. Those areas and ways that God wants to weed out of our behavior will be revealed as we go. We do not know all the self-centered places, wrong motives and bad attitudes that are hidden in our souls, but God is patient and gracious as He leads us on the path to intimacy with Him.

I personally remember when I made a "total surrender" to Jesus. It was in 1974. Some might speculate that I was not really saved at age nine and that the total surrender was the time I got saved. All I know is that when I surrendered, my life drastically changed. I went a little crazy to the point of taking all my regular novel-type books and giving them to the library. For about fifteen years I only read my Bible, books from the old saints or books to study the Bible. I have never been sorry that I surrendered to Jesus. I cannot imagine life without Him nor can I imagine how people go through difficult circumstances without Him.

Through the years, selling-out to Jesus did not prevent difficult circumstances. There were plenty. The difference was in how I walked through the difficulties. (We will look at Suffering and Trials in a later chapter.) Jesus learned obedience by the things He suffered, as will we. (Hebrews 5:8) But I have to say that there is no way to find true intimacy with Christ without a "total surrender."

Application: If you have never read the book, *Hinds' Feet on High Places,* I highly recommend it. The protagonist, Much Afraid, goes on a journey to find intimacy with the Shepherd (Jesus). He leads her away from her fear to total, surrendered love. Much Afraid tells the Shepherd, "Only have your will and way with me, Shepherd. Nothing else matters."[6] Think on these words.

"For God so loved the world that He gave His only begotten Son, that whoever believes in Him should not perish but have eternal life." John 3:16

I hope you have seen how much God loves you, and how secure you can be in His love. There are no words to describe it well enough. We can only try to imagine what it means to give one's only Son for a world that hardly cares most of the time. Stories of children lost for a short time give

---

[6] *Hinds' Feet on High Places,* Hannah Hurnard, Barbour and Company, Inc., Westwood, NJ, 1977, page128

us only a glimpse. If you have never received Christ, I encourage you to do so soon. If you are not certain of your salvation, consider the appropriate verses and ask God to show you. Truly understanding what salvation means is simple enough for children to make a response and complex enough to bring a lifetime of experience. Explore all facets of intimacy with Christ, beginning with salvation.

INTIMACY THROUGH GRACE AND UNION

"For by grace you have been saved through faith; and that not of yourselves, it is the gift of God; " - Ephesians 2:8

"As you therefore have received Christ Jesus the Lord, so walk in Him." Colossians 2:6

We looked at faith and salvation, the foundations of intimacy with Jesus, and we had a glimpse of the struggles involved in living by faith. It's one thing to receive Him as Savior and another to walk our journey with Him, but we do both the same way—by faith through grace. In my early struggles I did not really understand grace and how to walk in freedom. My mind was trained to believe that grace brought salvation, but the rest was up to me. I worked hard at doing right, but I also lived with worry.

I remember the first big crisis that came into my life. My third son, Greg, was born with what was then diagnosed as a terminal heart condition. There was nothing I could do to make it better. I did turn to God in my helplessness, but I did not know how to stop worrying and fretting. I continued to stumble along through the years, living life as it came, longing for the intimacy with God that I so often read about, but it eluded me because I carried the load. Intimacy through grace and union was missing from my experience.

Even after God miraculously healed my son's heart, I struggled with deep wounds from a trauma in my teen years that caused me to believe that I was a bad person in spite of the fact that I had received Christ. On the outside I could do the do's and not do the don'ts, but inside I harbored self-condemnation and rejection. The identity I had always lived out of was tainted by condemnation and performance-based teaching, an unclear view of God, and my own self-rejection based on years of lies that I believed about myself. I needed to hear a totally new message. I needed a different path, a path to freedom and acceptance. God brought me a new message and a new path. These are what this chapter is all about.

> *Application:* Are you carrying a load of worry and condemnation? Do you strive to be a good person but feel like a failure? God wants you to know Him and His truth that will set you free.

"He made Him who knew no sin to be sin on our behalf, that we might become the righteousness of God in Him." II Corinthians 5:21

I grew up in church, heard the Gospel nearly every Sunday, and received Christ at a very young age. When God brought the new message of grace and union to me, the first thing I discovered was that I only knew half of the Gospel—that I needed to receive Christ as my Savior and Lord. In this verse Paul gives us a deep, wonderful picture of the whole Gospel: *Jesus became sin so that we might become the righteousness of God.* But I only knew half of it—the half about Jesus. I had no clue what the other half meant nor did I understand many other verses I had memorized. The other half of the Gospel I was missing was about what happened to *me* on the Cross, how I could be righteous, and how that makes a difference in every-day life.

God began my journey to learn the other half of the Gospel in September, 1979, when I was on staff with Campus Crusade for Christ. I was sitting at my kitchen table with two new friends who asked me if I knew that, after becoming a Christian, the "old man" was gone. Because I had read several of the books my friends mentioned, I told them I did know that. After they left, their words continued to niggle at my mind, resulting in an inner dialogue full of questions such as, "Do I really know what they asked me?" "What does dying with Christ really mean?" "What does it matter?" "Will the tapes they left help me?"

> ***Application:*** If you have never heard before that the "old man," the "old self" is gone, keep reading. Part of the "Good News" is that you are no longer the old person you used to be.

"I have been crucified with Christ, and it is no longer I who live, but Christ lives in me; and the life which I now live in the flesh, I live by the faith of the Son of God who loved me and delivered Himself up for me." Galatians 2:20

After my new friends left, I got out my Bible and the Strong's Concordance to look up the verses they had quoted. After some study, I soon realized that what the friends had told me is true. "Okay," I said to myself, "I agree it's true, but I don't know what it means and why it matters." It would be months before I understood, but I continued to ponder and search and listen to cassette tapes by Dr. Bill Gillham,[7] which they'd left for me. I listened and read books and studied everything I could find, trying to make myself understand. It was exhausting. I didn't realize then that truth doesn't come through the intellect, but rather through revelation from God—so I was giving it all I had.

Finally, after we moved to Georgia in March, 1980, I began to get some light. I will never forget the day I saw by the Holy Spirit's revelation that, Yes! I died with Christ and that the rejected, worrying, condemned

---

[7] I will be sharing concepts I learned from these tapes. Years later, Bill and his wife Anabel wrote books that contain the same concepts. Where possible I will note the book and page numbers. Otherwise they will be from my memory of the tapes and lectures I heard in person.

identity that I had carried so long was really not true anymore. I nearly fell on my knees when He hit me with the truth. That was the beginning of a new path that would bring me more of the intimacy with Christ for which I longed. That journey has never ended.

> *Application:* If you find new truths here as you read, don't try to get them through memorizing, reasoning and logic. The truth has to be revealed by the Holy Spirit. Seek through your heart and be open to His leading and you will find new acceptance, love and freedom.

". . . but let it be the hidden person of the heart, with the imperishable quality of a gentle and quiet spirit, which is precious in the sight of God." 1 Peter 3:4

Learning who we are in Christ was my lifeline to understanding God's love, acceptance and freedom, but, what the Scriptures say about us does not always look and feel true in our experience. When that happens, we walk by faith. This came home to me one day in my prayer time. On the top of my personal list at that time was "Please, Lord, give me a gentle and quiet spirit." My personality type is not one of the more popular personalities, nor are my spiritual gifts—prophecy and discernment. It was easy to let that unpopularity influence how I looked at myself. Not being appreciated or accepted for my honesty contributed to my self-rejection, and I struggled to separate things that did need to be changed from things that needed to be accepted. I did not always distinguish between the two very well.

On this particular day I asked God again to please give me a gentle and quiet spirit. As I sat there, I heard Him speak quietly in my heart, *"You already have one. Now thank me for it."* I could not believe what I had heard! How could that be? How could I do that? "Not a chance," my emotions screamed. But deep inside my spirit I knew—Yes! That would be faith. Not only would it be faith (agreeing with God no matter what), but since it was His voice I was hearing, it would also be obedience. So I said aloud and wrote in my journal, "Thank you, Lord, that I have a gentle and quiet spirit." It was one of the most uncomfortable things I have ever done. It went against all my feelings and self-evaluations, but it was part of what I was learning about my new identity and walking in grace and freedom.

Did anyone else notice right away that I already had a gentle and quiet spirit? Not at all. Not for a very long time. But I had to say it was so from then on, walking by faith that what God says is true, NOT going by how I felt, looked, sounded, or acted. This was faith. This was pleasing to God. This was receiving His grace. It changed my life, not just because I made a choice, but because I heard God speak. The intimate relationship with Him is what changes us.

Looking at how we often have to walk out what God says versus going by what we are feeling or acting like brings us to an important part of intimacy through grace and union. We have to learn to separate personhood and behavior. Personhood is who we are both uniquely and in our spirits. Behavior is our actions, attitudes, and appearances. These two are not the same. The best way to see it is to ask yourself, "If I bark, am I a dog?" We will look more at the differences as we continue.

> ***Application:*** Is there a characteristic that you long to have real in your life? By faith, claim that it is already true about you because of Christ. Don't look to your behavior for proof. Look to Him and what He says. Ask and listen for His perspective.

"Now may the God of peace Himself sanctify you entirely and may your spirit and soul and body be preserved complete, without blame at the coming of our Lord Jesus Christ." 1 Thessalonians 5:23

In order to help us separate personhood and behavior and understand other things Jesus did on the Cross besides save us from our sins, it will be easier if we see that we humans are a spirit, we have a soul and we live in a body. There are various ways to describe these parts and sometimes the descriptions cause controversy, but for our purposes here, we will look at them this way:

Part One: The Human Spirit: "the real us," "the heart"

When I speak of the human spirit, it will mean the part of us that is the "real us." The human spirit is sometimes referred to as the "heart." The heart is like the eyes and ears we have towards God where we hear His voice for guidance, conviction and loving comments. It is the place inside of us in which the Holy Spirit comes to live after we receive Jesus. I Corinthians 6 tells us in verse 17, "He who joins himself to the Lord is one spirit with Him," and in verse 19, "Or do you not know that your body is a temple of the Holy Spirit who is in you, whom you have from God, and that you are not your own?"

Before the Holy Spirit comes to live in us, the human spirit is "dead to God." God told Adam and Eve if they ate the fruit, they would die. They did not die physically at that moment, they died spiritually. They lost their innocence with God. Ephesians 2:1 says, "And you were dead in your trespasses and sins." When our human spirit is united with the Holy Spirit, we are alive to God. "But God, being rich in mercy, because of His great love with which He loved us, even when were dead in our transgressions, made us alive together with Christ. . ." Ephesians 2: 4-5

Part Two: The Soul: where we think, feel and choose

The soul is where we think, feel and choose. It is our personality; the place where we interact with others. The soul is damaged by things that happened to us when we were growing up. The mind believes lies about who we are and who God is; the feelings we have are extreme and/or stuck in immaturity, and our wills can be stubborn and selfish. This is the part that God works on to help us grow and relate better. For example, many people have grown up being told that they are stupid, clumsy, ugly, worthless, inadequate or unwanted. These messages can be given verbally and non-verbally. However they are given, such messages wound us and we believe they are true, when God says they are not true.

I have talked to many people through the years like Ann and John. Ann grew up in a home that was full of anger and chaos. Ann's mother blamed some of her struggles on Ann and often said, "I wish you had never been born." On the other hand, John was not told bluntly that he was a problem, but because there was no room for failure in his family, John believed he was worthless and could not do anything right. Some children are just ignored and neglected; others are outright abused. These are examples of wounds to the soul that lead to believing the opposite of what God says about His beloved, delighted in, valuable, wanted children.

Part Three: The Body: "the earth suit"

Dr. Bill Gillham, the dear teacher I was introduced to via cassettes and who is now with Jesus, called our bodies an earth suit.[8] Bodies are only suitable for earth. They help us get around, interact with others and accomplish things that we need to do for every-day living. They connect with our feelings and thoughts to make life more interesting and full. Our bodies will not go to Heaven. We will need a new one, a resurrected one, for that.

As we look at intimacy through grace and union, in order to understand all that Christ did on the Cross and what it means for us, we will distinguish these "three parts." It will also be helpful to answer some questions such as, "Who am I?" "Why do I talk about myself in different ways?" "Who is the 'I' in this verse?" "What does it mean to be 'in'

---

[8] *Lifetime Guarantee*, Harvest House Publishers, Eugene, Oregon, 97402, 1993, pages 71-72

someone?" Much of what we will look at is on a spiritual level, but here and there the spiritual and physical will both be involved.

"I" is both spiritual (the spirit part of us) and physical (the soul personality and body.) Most often we mix these together without thinking about it at all. It can be helpful to distinguish; although in truth, "I am me, a whole person."

One reason for distinguishing our "three parts" is in order to learn some of the things God says about us that are true spiritually, but we may not understand them or be experiencing them. If one is not experiencing what God says is true, then it's easy to think it's not true—and throw the baby out with the bathwater. For example, God says we are accepted in Christ, but if like Ann and John whom we looked at earlier, rejection was the main form of interaction we learned, acceptance will be a foreign truth, especially at times when we behave badly. "I," the real me, the spirit part of me, is accepted in the Beloved whether I behave that way or not. Like any good parent, God will correct behavior without condemning His child. He will remember who the child is; He will separate personhood and behavior.

As we dissect the spirit-soul-body and look at who is "I," another "I" we use is the soul part, our unique personality that makes us different from others. God loves this "I" very much, too, and He skillfully made each one of us as different as snowflakes and fingerprints. Unfortunately in our fallen world, the soul gets damaged when hurt and not comforted. People with damaged souls believe lies that cause behavior problems, further confusing how we look at what is true about us in the spiritual realm. We live out of what we believe. (Proverbs 23:7) For example, if we look down and see a rattlesnake by our foot, we will feel great fear and try to run. Our emotions and our behavior will look like what we believe. In a moment, we find out that the snake is made of rubber. Now we believe something else, and although our emotions may still be high, the behavior will change.[9] Behavior works the same way with spiritual knowledge. We may know lots of scripture, but what we truly believe in our heart at a given moment will determine our behavior. One important result of

---

[9] Rattlesnake story from Bill Gillham, *Lifetime Guarantee*, pages 21-22

knowing this principle is that it helps us see that *we* are not bad—*it's the lie that we believe that is tripping us up.* As Christians, in our spirits we do not need to change. We are A-Okay there. It's what we believe that needs to change.

I have a friend who was told growing up that he was stupid and would never amount to much. In spite of the fact that he earned a college degree in engineering and had a successful career, for years, deep inside, he believed he was stupid and inadequate. Those beliefs showed up in his family relationships and his verbal evaluations of himself. He would not try to do hard tasks around the house and continually felt like a failure. It was not until he learned who he is in Christ that he stopped putting himself down and began to branch out and try new things. Like the rattlesnake story, my friend acted out what he felt and believed to be true.

Application: Is there something you believe about yourself that does not correlate with what God says about you? Replace that with His truth by interacting with Him about it. What wrong messages were you given growing up that God needs to change? Let God show you so that He can replace those lies with His truth and with intimacy with Him.

"I have been crucified with Christ, and it is no longer I who live, but Christ lives in me; and the life which I now live in the flesh, I live by the faith of the Son of God who loved me and delivered Himself up for me." Galatians 2:20

When we receive Christ into our hearts, many new things become true about us. We will look at these as we go along, truths such as being crucified with Christ, raised with Christ, seated in the heavenly places with Him, holy, righteous, blameless, accepted, loved and wanted.[10] We will continue to look at verses about who we are in Christ so that we can realize that these attributes are really true and not just something God says that will be true in the future after we go to Heaven.

Christ has joined Himself to us in our spirits, has come to live in us, and He wants to live His life through us, as us. This means that we have the choice to turn to Him and give Him our struggles and hurts and allow Him to work things out in His way and time. It means we can stop worrying; it means we have to exercise faith and trust and keep clinging to Him even when things do not appear to be working out. It means, for example, if we feel anxious, we recognize that Christ's character is one of peace, so we turn to Him to find out about our anxiety. Or when it's difficult to love someone, we recognize that He is love and turn to Him to love that person through us. When we see His perspective on our troubles, we experience Him as our peace or our love. This brings rest. What a relief to leave our worries in God's hands.

> *Application:* What worries do you need to put into God's hands? Where do you need to let Jesus live through you? It is He who lives His life in and through you, not your exhausting self-effort.

". . . and raised us up with Him and seated us with Him in the heavenly places in Christ Jesus." Ephesians 2:6

"If then *(since) you* have been raised up with Christ, keep seeking the things above, where Christ is seated at the right hand of God." Colossians 3:1 *(Emphasis mine.)*

---

[10] Holy, righteous, blameless from *Lifetime Guarantee*, pages 91, 125-127, 131

Not only are we crucified, buried and resurrected in Christ, we are also seated with Him in the heavenly places. When we think about that, it helps us have a different perspective on our circumstances. Not only is He here with us and in us, we are in His lap at the right hand of the Father. Does it always feel like that's true? Certainly not. But it is true, and we have the choice to take it and believe it—or not. When we do believe that we are seated with Jesus, we'll look down on our circumstances from His lap instead of seeing them larger than life.

> ***Application:*** Is there a circumstance in your life that you need to look at from the perspective of Jesus' lap? You're there with Him; He's here with you, and He wants to comfort you and give you His perspective.

"In that day you will know that I am in My Father, and you in Me, and I in you." John 14:20

"Therefore if anyone is in Christ, he is a new creature; the old things passed away; behold, new things have come." 2 Corinthians 5:17

"And, so to speak, through Abraham, even Levi, who received tithes, paid tithes, for he was still in the loins of his father when Melchizedek met him." Hebrews 7:9-10

Sitting in the heavenly places with Jesus is just part of what it means to be "in Christ," a phrase Paul uses numerous times in the books of Ephesians and Colossians. The author of Hebrews gives us here an easy way to see it. Abraham met the priest Melchizedek and paid tithes to him. Hebrews tells us that Levi, who was not yet born, also paid the tithes to

Melchizedek. He did so because he was "in Abraham." Whatever happened to Abraham happened to Levi. Whatever was true of Abraham was true of Levi. Just as Levi was "in Abraham's loins," we are in Christ.

> *Application:* Don't panic if this feels mysterious. It's a life-changing truth. Take time to ponder. We will look at it some more.

"For since by a man came death, by a man also came the resurrection of the dead. For as in Adam all die, so also in Christ all shall be made alive." 1Corinthians 15:21-22

"Therefore, just as through one man sin entered into the world, and death through sin, and so death spread to all men, because all sinned." Romans 5:12

"Or do you not know that all of us who have been baptized into Christ Jesus have been baptized into His death? Therefore we have been buried with Him through baptism into death, in order that as Christ was raised from the dead through the glory of the Father, so we too might walk in newness of life." Romans 6: 3-4

Go back and read these verses again as you continue to consider what it means to be "in Christ." In the Corinthians verse we see that we were in someone else before we were in Christ. We were in Adam. One Romans verse tells us the consequences of being in Adam—death. The other Romans verses tell us that when we became a Christian we were "baptized" into Christ. The Greek word for baptism gives the picture of something immersed into something else, like sugar into coffee. They cannot be separated. (Technically, they could be separated in a lab, but for our purposes here, think about it as if you had a cup of coffee in front of you.) At salvation, we are put into Christ so that, like Levi, whatever happened to Christ happened to us and whatever is true of Christ is true of us. So we died with Him, were buried with Him and were raised with Him. When you understand this great happening, you will see yourself the way God does. Seeing yourself through God's eyes will bring freedom and rest.

Let's examine more closely what it means to be "in Adam" or "in Christ." All humans are born being "in Adam." We are sinners because we are born sinners in Adam, not just because we sin. We sin because we are sinners, not the other way around as most of us have been taught. If we had been in the Garden of Eden we would have sinned exactly as Adam did—we would have eaten the forbidden fruit. Because we were "in him, in his loins," what happened to him happened to us—we died spiritually. What was true of him was true of us—we lost our relationship with God and became separated from Him. This is why we need to die with Christ and be born again. *We need a completely new lineage.* When we receive Christ, God gives us that new lineage in Him. Now what happened to Christ—His death, burial, resurrection and ascension—happened to us spiritually, and even more wonderful to ponder and take is that whatever is true of Christ is true of us, in our personhood, the spiritual part of us. We are holy, righteous, accepted, loved, delighted in, adequate, free—and the list goes on....

Baptized and crucified go together. Because we are immersed into Christ, all that happened to Him happened to us. That is how we can be crucified, buried, raised and seated with Him. Water baptism is a symbolic picture of that immersion—death, burial and resurrection to a new life.

Application: Do you realize that you have the attributes of Christ in your inner most being? They may not show up all the time in your behavior, but they are there. You have a new lineage, a new past, a new life. You are holy, righteous and blameless. Think on these things.

"Knowing this that our <u>old self</u> was crucified with Him, that our body of sin might be done away with that we should no longer be slaves to sin; for who he who has died is freed from sin." Romans 6:6-7 *(emphasis mine)*

"I have been crucified with Christ, and it is no longer I who live, but Christ lives in me; and the life which I now live in the flesh (body) I live by the faith of the Son of God who loved me and delivered Himself up for me." Galatians 2:20

It's very important to note some different words in the Greek in order to understand what was crucified and what was raised with Christ. "Old self, old nature, and old man" are translated in various versions from the Greek word *anthropos*. We see here in these two verses that our "*anthropos,*" our old self, has been crucified and buried with Christ. The Romans verse uses that Greek word. Our old self is the part of us that was separated from God because of Adam's sin and being in him. It is gone. After conversion, we have a new self, a new creation, joined to Christ as one. (2 Corinthians 5:17)

On the other hand we still have a condition that some versions call the flesh or the sinful nature—*sarx* or *sark* in the Greek. Two examples are Romans 8:6, "For the mind set on the flesh is death, but the mind set on the Spirit is life and peace," and Galatians 5:16, "But I say walk by the Spirit and you will not carry out the desire of the flesh." In some older versions of the *New International Version,* they use *sinful nature* in both verses where NASB and KJV use *flesh.*

In passages where *sark* is translated "sinful nature," this can be misleading, as most people associate "nature" with the words translated from *anthropos*—old man, old nature. It's easier to understand the distinctions when keeping in mind that nature and flesh are two different words in the Greek with two different purposes and places in our lives. In order to understand all that happened on the Cross, it's good to remember that the "old you that could not be with God" (*anthropos*, old man) died with Christ and you *are* a new creation in your spirit. But because of sin in the world and lies you believe, you can *act* differently than who God says you are, because you can choose to lean on your own understanding apart from God—(*sark,* flesh, sinful nature) (Proverbs 3: 5-6)

On a practical level, separating *anthropos (old man)* from the *sark (flesh)* will help us understand how not to lean on our own understanding and to remember that we need Jesus every moment to show us His way. Knowing the "old us" died helps us relate better to God, others and ourselves because we experience His love and acceptance, making it easier to love and accept others. The new creation lives by the faith of the Son of God who now lives in us in the person of the Holy Spirit. We have a different perspective on life because Christ is now our new life.

Look at the following diagram from Dr. Charles Solomon for another way to see what we are considering:[11]

DIAGRAM 9

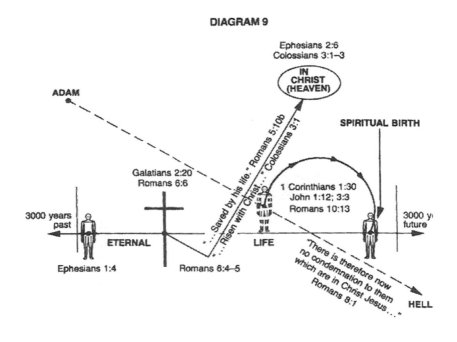

---

[11] From *Handbook to Happiness*, Tyndale House Publishers, Inc. Wheaton, Illinois, 1971; page 40; used with permission

Application: Take some time to study the diagram and look up all the verses. This will help you as you go through this chapter and the next one on Law and Grace. Ask Jesus to reveal what these truths mean for you.

"Blessed be the God and Father of our Lord Jesus Christ who has blessed us with every spiritual blessing in the heavenly places in Christ. Just as He chose us in Him before the foundation of the world, that we should be holy and blameless before Him. In love He predestined us to adoption as sons through Jesus Christ to Himself, according to the kind intention of His will." Ephesians 1:3-5 (NASB)

"To the praise of the glory of His grace wherein He hath made us accepted in the Beloved." Ephesians 1:6 (KJV)

"Do not be conformed to this world, but be transformed by the renewing of your mind, that you may prove what the will of God is, that which is good and acceptable and perfect." Romans 12:1

Part One

Being "holy and blameless" and "accepted in the Beloved," are just a few of the blessings we have because we are in Christ. Ephesians and Colossians are full of verses that contain the words "in Him," or "in Christ." We are often taught that Christ is in us, but not so often taught that we are in Him, much less what all that means. Remember holy, blameless and accepted are things that are true about us, the "real us," in our spirits, not always in our behavior.

Part Two

If it sounds too good to be true that we who we are in Christ are holy, righteous, blameless, loved and accepted, it will help us understand if we "take it." By "take it" I don't mean just reading a verse one time and thinking about its meaning. So what do I mean by "take it?"

Years ago I understood "taking something" when I met Norman Grubb, a British writer and speaker who is now with Jesus. Norman spoke several times in my home. I loved it when Norman talked about faith and how to get the truth into our experience. He said many times, "What you take, takes you," illustrating what he meant by reminding us how, after eating an apple, the apple becomes part of us. He often illustrated by reminding us how we learn a new job or a new skill. At first we have to think about the new job or skill, we have to practice the different aspects, make notes, ask questions of someone who knows the skill already, until one day, what we have "taken" has taken us. Now we say, "I *am* a carpenter. I *am* a teacher. I *am* a baseball player."

In his book, *Lifetime Guarantee,* Dr. Gillham describes his version of "taking the truth" in conjunction with "setting your mind" (Colossians 3:2). As we take the truth and set our minds on things above, we are doing what Romans 12:2 says—renewing our minds. He says if we set our mind on the truth several times a day that leave less time for setting it on negative things which are "death." What happens to our negative pathways is similar to what happens to our high school algebra—we forget it. We don't fight the negative; we set our minds on the positive.[12]

Part Three

As we consider the truths we sometimes need to take by faith, let's look at verb tenses in some verses. After learning that I am in Christ and what that means, I began re-reading my Bible in a way that felt as if I'd never read the New Testament before. I began noticing verb tenses and how many of them are past tense. For example these verses from Ephesians: (Italics mine)   "He *has blessed* us with every spiritual

---

[12] *Lifetime Guarantee*, page 133

blessing," " . . .you *were sealed* in Him with the Holy Spirit of promise," "you *were dead* in your trespasses and sin, in which you *formerly walked*," ". . . *made* us alive together with Christ . . .. *raised* us up with Him and *seated* us in the Heavenly places in Christ Jesus." Then from Colossians: "in Him you *have been made* complete," "you *were* also circumcised with a circumcision made without hands," "having *canceled* out the certificate of debt . . .He *has taken* it out of the way," "Since you *have died* with Christ," "for you *have died* and your life is hidden with Christ in God."

These are some of the truths that we want to take by faith until they become real in our experience. Taking what is true is not the power of positive thinking—these things are really true about us. We may not feel like they're true; we may not always act like they're true, but they are true if we're in Christ.

As we learn new truths and begin to take them, we're taking something that is true, not trying to make it true by saying it. Remember, when you're taking a truth such as, "I am holy," based on Ephesians 1: 4, you take it because it is already true about the real you in your spirit. Remember when God told me to thank Him for my gentle and quiet spirit that I didn't feel like I had, and others may have agreed? I had to write it out, thank God and then tell some friends, "God says I already have a gentle and quiet spirit." Through the years, as I consistently thanked God and "took" what He said was true, the reality in my behavior of a gentle and quiet spirit caught up with what I took.

> ***Application:*** What negative thoughts do you need to let go of and replace with positive ones? What are some of God's truths that you need to "take until they take you?"

"Even so consider yourselves to be dead to sin, but alive to God in Christ Jesus." Romans 6: 11

"Therefore do not let sin reign in your mortal body that you should obey its lusts, and do not go on presenting the members of your body to sin as instruments of unrighteousness, but present yourself to God as those alive from the dead and your members as instruments of righteousness to God." Romans 6: 12-13

After hearing that Christians are holy, righteous and blameless, the question always arises: "Then why do I still sin?" Romans 6, 7 and 8 help us see how to look at sin. In these verses, we see that we are no longer slaves to sin. A dead person is no longer a slave to the old master. The old self is gone; we are alive to God. The old self, *the anthropos*, is gone. When I first heard that the old self was gone, I asked myself, "So what? How does that make anything different?" And like most, I wondered, "Then why do I still sin?" I hope the answers to these questions will become evident as we move through more verses.

I used to think that I was prone to sin because, even as a Christian, inside I had a "white dog" who was good, probably Jesus, and a "black dog" who was bad. These were at war and it was up to me to "feed" the white dog and see that the good dog won so I would not sin. I don't believe that old story any more. If Jesus is the white dog then I have to be the black dog. That makes me bad. When I believed I am essentially bad, that's how I lived. Maybe not sinning all the time, but there were huge amounts of self-rejection going on inside. Now if my behavior stinks, I remind myself that I am a new creation in Christ. (II Corinthians 5:17) The behavior has to be addressed, but I am not bad.

Knowing that the old self is gone makes it easier to "not let sin reign in my body." If the part of us is gone to which we have always attributed our "badness," we focus less on sin and less on trying to be better in our own efforts. We live like who we believe we are. In his book, *Birthright: Christian Do You Know Who You Are?* David Needham tells a story about a young man whose principle focus was on food and girls. His coach thought he was a sprinter and challenged him to train. As the weeks went by, the boy began to recognize that he was built to run and loved it. When a girl tempted him with a big piece of pie and a date with her, the young man turned her down in no uncertain terms, "I'm a sprinter. That's who I am."[13] He resisted sin because he knew who he was.

Just like the young sprinter, when we know who God says we are—holy, righteous, blameless, and accepted—we will sin less because we will live out of who we know we are. It might seem to some that the freedom this brings would cause us to sin more easily, but in truth we sin less, because our focus is on Jesus and how much He loves us instead of worrying whether we are good enough to have that deep intimacy we want with Him. When I believed down deep in my soul that I was unworthy, unlovable, and unable to do much of anything right, Jesus was often at arm's length—not because He held me off, but because I did not understand His love and acceptance. I carried guilt that had been forgiven; I had myself under the Law when He had freed me from the Law. I could not snuggle up in His lap. After understanding all that happened on the Cross, when I was tempted to believe no one loved me, in my mind I would say, "Stop! That is not true! I am loved and accepted in the Beloved, just as I am."

> ***Application:*** Do you know who you are? Do you still believe you are partly a white dog and a black dog? Ask Jesus to show you the differences and why they are important. He wants you to know that you are loved and accepted and free. He wants you to be able to snuggle up in His lap.

---

[13] David Needham *Birthright: Christian Do You Know Who You Are?*, Multnomah Publishers, Sisters, OR, 1979, pages 91-93

"Or do you not know, brethren (for I am speaking to those who know the law), that the law has jurisdiction over a person as long as he lives? For the married woman is bound by the law to her husband while he is living; but if her husband dies, she is released from the law concerning him. So then if, while her husband is living, she is joined to another man, she shall be called an adulteress; but if her husband dies, she is free from the law so that she is not an adulteress, though she is joined to another man." Romans 7: 1-3

"Therefore, my brethren, you also were made to die to the Law through the body of Christ, that you might be joined to another, to Him who was raised from the dead, that we might bear fruit for God." Romans 7: 4

Verses from Romans 7: 1-3 are often shared as an objection to divorce and remarriage. Taken in context with chapters 6 and 8, they are not about divorce at all. They are about being free from the Law. Look at verse four again. Notice who it is that dies. In verse two, the husband dies and the wife is free. But who dies in verse four? You died. I died.

So we may ask, "Why did we die?" "What difference does it make?" Our old husband, the Law is not going to die; the Law is good and holy. So *we* had to die in order to be free. We had to die in order to be joined to another. Now we are joined to Christ. We are freed from the Law. The Law was our first husband, the old life apart from God.

Application: Are you getting to know your "new husband?" He does not condemn; He is not a heavy-handed master. He loves you dearly. Remember this: Who you love determines your identity.[14]

---

[14] E. James Wilder, et. al., *Joy Starts Here*, Shepherd's House, Inc., East Peoria, IL, 61611, 2013, page 215.

"For the good that I wish, I do not do, but I practice the very evil that I do not wish. But if I am doing the very thing I do not wish, I am no longer the one doing it, but sin which dwells in me." Romans 7: 19-20

This passage helps us continue looking for answers to the question, "Why do I still sin?" Every Christian feels the pull described here. Many have taught that the pull is a sign of our badness, even after becoming a Christian. Upon closer observation it seems to say the opposite; it *proves we are* a Christian: I want to do *good*. I do not want to do evil. But there is something keeping me from doing the good I want to do. This dilemma often leads to self-hatred, especially with a Christian who wants to please God; because many of us have been taught growing up that we can "only do bad things." The following are excerpts from *Jewels for My Journey* during a time when I was going through difficult circumstances. My counselor, Dr. Jim Wilder, helped me look at this famous passage differently.

> This is the ideal: Suppose you had a baby and dropped him and banged his head. Your immediate response is to move close and comfort. This is the normal way. At some age, most people learn to get angry and push away from the one that hurt them. If you really hurt them and they won't let you close, then you hate yourself. Self-hatred is a response to powerlessness—you can make bad things happen but not good things. As long as you believe inside that bad things are all you can make happen, you will hate yourself. First you feel frustration at doing a bad thing, then you try to get close to someone you hurt, and if the other gets more upset, it gets worse and worse down to self-hatred. This is such a horrible view of our humanity.

The popular belief about Romans 7 is "I can only do bad things" If you think you are bad and can only do bad things, you will think it's going to feel better if you do bad things to yourself—like beat up on yourself. The thinking is that you are at least doing bad things to the right person—yourself.

> If we consider ourselves to be bad after causing someone pain, then if we cause anyone pain we automatically feel we are bad, and we stand condemned. Causing pain is not always bad. Dentists cause pain to make a rotten tooth feel better. Doctors cause pain with surgery to fix a disease. God and good parents cause pain to help their children grow well. Telling someone the truth can cause pain. (We will look closely at wrong beliefs about pain in the chapter on Suffering and Trials.) [15]

This common struggle to think we are bad and beat up on ourselves can seem confusing and complex. How often do we say something hurtful to a family member or friend and immediately think, "I always mess up!" Is the struggle we feel when we mess up because of what some call the "old self?" (*anthropos*) Is it the sinful nature, the flesh? (*sark*) Or is it something else? And where does the struggle take place?

Application: Have you been taught that Romans 7 is a sign that you mostly do bad things? Do you often feel this struggle inside? Stay open to seeing these passages in a different light that will help you know who you are in Christ.

---

[15] From *Jewels for My Journey* pages 159-160

"For I joyfully concur with the law of God in the inner man, but I see a different law in the members of my body, waging war against the law of my mind and making me a prisoner of the law of sin which is in my members." Romans 7: 22-23

Now Paul tells us that the struggle—to do what we want and not do what we don't want—is in the body and the mind. The inner man (the new *anthropos* united with Christ in our spirit) loves to keep God's law. The battle is in the mind, the soul, against the law of sin in the body. It is not I, the new me, who has the problem, it is the "law of sin," or as Bill Gillham and Dr. Solomon call it, the "power of sin" that causes me problems.[16] The struggle comes from the old lies that I learned growing up and still believe. The "law of sin" is like a splinter in my finger—it's in me, but it's not me. It causes me problems because of unhealed painful memories and lies that get triggered by present circumstances that feel similar to old events from the past—but it is not me.

Let's look at an example: Last year at a family gathering, I tried to help someone in my family and when I asked them a question they growled sarcastically at me. Being growled at for seemingly no reason brought up shame and hurt inside and I began to shut down. Shutting down is not what I want to do in this kind of situation. The feeling is like a pull back and forth to retaliate or to go silent, neither the best response. Lies about my unworthiness swirled as I felt like a victim. It took a few minutes to turn to Jesus and reset my heart so that I could remember who I really am and that I do not want to shut someone out, harbor resentment and/or bite back at anyone. I also chose to look at the other person and see their heart and how circumstances were affecting them. I chose not to listen to my old feelings of being a victim. I escaped the Romans 7 dilemma by turning to Jesus, looking at who I am, and doing what is like me to do.

Here is another example of a more "outward sin." Recently I felt anger at a friend over something she said and I did lash out at her. I was instantly sorry for lashing out, but it took a few minutes for my anger to subside. In the past before knowing God's grace and my union with Christ, I would

---

[16] *Lifetime Guarantee*, page 80

have beaten up on myself quite extensively for hurting someone like that. But now I process my sin quite differently because I know how to separate my actions from my personhood. I confessed the sin to God, agreeing I did not act like myself and I sought forgiveness from my friend. The big difference is that I do not beat up on myself for failing because I separate the law of sin from who I really am. I used to beat up on myself all the time because deep down I thought I was bad and could only do bad things. Freedom comes from knowing it is not me, the new me, doing these things but a temporary belief in a lie about who I am and/or who God is. (More to come on this in the chapter on Feelings and Appearances.)

> ***Application:*** Do you beat up on yourself when you mess up? God does not want you to do that. It can be a hard habit to break, but worth the effort to appropriate these truths. Think on these truths—that you are in Christ, that *you* are not the problem; it's what you believe that needs to change. Get healing for emotional wounds and lies that keep you from experiencing intimacy.

"Wretched man that I am! Who will set me free from the body of this death? Thanks be to God through Jesus Christ our Lord! So then, on the one hand I myself with my mind am serving the law of God, but on the other, with my flesh the law of sin." Romans 7:24-25

Now we are getting closer to the answer about sin. Our struggles are connected to our earthly bodies, our misdirected minds and our damaged emotions. The picture here in this verse is of a murderer with his victim's dead body tied to his body—arms to arms, legs to legs. In Paul's time criminals actually had to carry that rotting body of death of the one that they had murdered until it killed them as well. Figuratively speaking, today we might find ourselves carrying "dead bodies" of guilt and condemnation in the form of addictions. Unhealed painful memories weigh us down and fear of failure or bad habits defeat us. Even carrying around memories of some sin we have done repeatedly can make it hard for us to believe we can make a better choice. The enemy accesses those memories in our minds and tells us there is no hope of change.

But there *is* hope; glorious hope. Paul answers the dilemma in the same verse: Jesus Christ our Lord has already done all that was needed to set us free. Christ has set us free from the "body of death." When the Romans 7 struggle comes, by faith we take the truth and turn to Him so that he can make the truth real in our experience. We have been set free. If we speak harshly to someone, we ask forgiveness from them and God, and then we take the truth that we are forgiven and there is no condemnation. If we feel inadequate, we turn to Jesus and take that He has made us complete in Him (Colossians 2:10). If we feel fearful, we turn to Jesus and take that He has "not given us a spirit of fear, but of power and love and a sound mind." (2 Timothy 1:7 KJV) If we feel unloved, we take the truth that Jesus loves us. If we feel anxious, we take that He is our peace. (Ephesians 2:14)

We can't turn to Jesus in our own strength and self-effort. It's very easy to forget His promises and how much He loves us when emotions are high and/or we have sinned once again. Sometimes we need "Jesus with skin on" in the form of a friend who can help us remember the truth. Part of the faith journey to intimacy is falling down and getting back up. We have to *practice* the new ways of looking at ourselves and God. We have to learn that we can't crucify ourselves. Instead we count it true that our old life is *already* dead and we are free. (Romans 6:11) Jesus wants to live His life through us. We may have to do some work on healing old lies and triggers, (more on that later) but on the journey there is no place for believing lies, taking condemnation, or indulging in self-hatred.

Application: Think about how you need others to help you during distress. Do you have someone? Do you ask for and allow others to help? Open up and exercise faith in what God says. The Lord Jesus Christ has set you free from the body of death. Trust and obey.

"There is therefore, no condemnation for those who are in Christ Jesus. For the law of the Spirit of life in Christ Jesus has set you free from the law of sin and death." Romans 8:1

Learning this verse about "no condemnation" and that God loves me unconditionally and wants to live His life through me has lessened the burden that made me believe I had to perform perfectly, fix everything and carry burdens that were not mine. It was common for me to beat up on myself for something as insignificant as burning the toast at dinner. "No condemnation" carried over to others as well when they didn't perform perfectly. Christ Jesus has already made the path to such freedom that results in no longer rejecting oneself and others. When the lights come on —we see that Jesus has done all and changed everything! Just as an airplane overcomes the law of gravity with the law of aerodynamics, the law of the Spirit has set us free from the law of sin and death. The law of gravity and the law of sin and death are still there, but they have no power when the other laws are followed. Every tiny bit of condemnation, whether at ourselves or others, must be rejected. There is no condemnation for those in Christ Jesus. We are accepted in the Beloved. (Ephesians 1:6 KJV) There may be discipline, but there is no condemnation.

I remember the time that I was going through my divorce. That was a period of my life where I struggled greatly to combat thoughts that turned to condemnation. Divorce is a hot topic for pointing fingers and emphasizing failure. I was terribly misunderstood and accused of wrongs such as having a pity party or making mountains out of molehills. No matter how I walked through that time there would be painful consequences for many people. I had to have help from others to remember who I was and not take or give condemnation. As I clung to Jesus, I struggled, but I clung to His word that I am accepted in the Beloved. Sometimes it was difficult to take the truth, but constant reminders kept my mind focused on Jesus. His presence was real, comforting and validating. Tapping into His presence during the pain I was going through was instrumental in my journey to intimacy with Him.

As I struggled through this difficult time, I knew that choosing to condemn and reject myself or others would only serve to make things worse. Pain can be borne without condemning ourselves or others when we understand that pain is not bad, we are not bad for having or causing pain, and we have comfort when feeling it. (The ideas about pain here do not apply to abuse or meanness. We'll see more on the way to view pain in the chapter on Suffering and Trials.)

Consequences can be paid without condemnation when we accept that God loves us no matter what we do. His love never changes, though our choices may bring consequences. Divorce hurts everyone concerned— family, community, church—everyone. But divorce is not an unforgiveable sin. The painful and uprooting consequences are terrible, but we do not have to add condemnation to all the pain. The law of the Spirit overcomes the law of sin and death as we cling to God and walk through the valley with Him. When we believe in His love, keep turning to Him in the pain and do not give or take any condemnation, a terrible consequence will have less meanness and hostility, making a very difficult road a little better.

Application: Is there something for which you find yourself taking condemnation? Do you try to be a perfectionist in order to feel okay about yourself? Begin to say, "Stop!" as soon as you catch yourself taking self-condemnation. Jesus has changed everything so you can be free.

"For what the Law could not do, weak as it was through the flesh, God did, sending His own Son in the likeness of sinful flesh and as an offering for sin, He condemned sin in the flesh, in order that the requirement of the Law might be fulfilled in us, who do not walk according to the flesh, but according to the Spirit." Romans 8: 3-4

If performing well and doing everything right could have saved us, Jesus would not have had to come. (I Corinthians 15: 14, 17) Just as we cannot keep the Law well enough to save ourselves, we cannot keep it after we are saved. When we try to keep the Law in our own strength via the flesh, we will fail. Keeping the Law in us *after* salvation is Jesus' job, too. Not only does He save us, He fulfills His requirements in us as we trust Him and listen to Him and let Him work.

As we go through life, we have the choice to walk according to the flesh or the Spirit. For example, sometimes I feel tempted to retaliate when someone hurts me. Retaliating would be walking according to the flesh, the *sark.* Remember the flesh tells me I know how to figure out what is best without listening to God. In this scenario the flesh would likely give me thoughts something like: "You hurt me—I'll hurt you back." Here I have the choice to listen to retaliatory thoughts or turn to the Spirit. Jesus says to love our neighbors and even our enemies, so I can say to Him something like, "I am not feeling much love right now for this person, but I want Your love to come through me to them so that we can resolve our problems with patience and kindness." Turning to Him for Him to live through me is walking according to the Spirit. The Spirit is our power source when we allow Him to work. He has to keep the commandment in us for it to be sincere and real.

Application: To whom are you listening when distress comes? Begin to turn to Jesus so that you can walk according to the Spirit. Your relationship with Him is what makes it possible.

"For those who are according to the flesh set their minds on the things of the flesh, but those who are according to the Spirit the things of the Spirit. For the mind set on the flesh is death, but the mind set on the Spirit is life and peace." Romans 8: 5-6

"Set your mind on the things above, not on things that are on earth." Colossians 3:2

As we continue in Romans, it will be helpful to look more closely at the word "according" in these verses. "Agreeing" is another meaning of "according." We could also substitute the word "focusing." Flesh is very self-centered, worldly, materialistic, sneaky and un-teachable. When we focus on the flesh, our bodies, the material world, or what we think is the right thing to do, death is the result. Death takes many forms besides the physical. Death can be the consequences of bad choices or the loss of valued relationships. The opposite of death is life and peace. Life satisfies and brings joy, even in difficult circumstances. When we focus on the Spirit, it's easier to think of others and their needs and be willing to listen when we need correction. Peace reigns when our focus is on the things of the Spirit.

As Paul continues contrasting the flesh versus the Spirit here, he makes his case a little stronger by telling us that not only do we have a choice to walk according to the flesh or the Spirit, we have a choice where we set our minds. The two are very similar because they both involve our focus. When we get *stuck* focusing on the flesh it seems to be a bit more than just walking along and getting irritated and wanting to retaliate. It seems to be more like a lifestyle. Some people might call setting our minds on the flesh "having a negative mindset," or "stirring garbage," or "worrying." Setting our minds on the Spirit can be a lifestyle, too. It does not mean that we only read our Bibles and pray, but rather that we keep turning to Jesus when the negatives, fears, doubts and worries enter our minds. The more we think on good things when circumstances are normal, the easier it will be to remember them when negatives arise.

> ***Application:*** Think on these truths throughout the day when circumstances are normal and not intense, so that when difficulties come, you will be more likely to remember the truth.

"Finally, brethren, whatever is true, whatever is honorable, whatever is right, whatever is true, whatever is lovely, whatever is of good repute, if there is any excellence and if anything worthy of praise, let your mind dwell on these things." Philippians 4:8

Here we see Paul's emphasis on setting our minds on the good things when circumstances are normal. We want these excellent and worthy things to be our focus so that when negatives arise, we are more likely to respond in love and kindness. Recently my 5 year-old grandson, Ryan, tracked mud into the house and onto the carpet. My daughter, Jodi, and I both responded kindly to his mistake instead of blowing up on him. We make it a practice to look at life the way Paul says in this verse so that when someone blows it, we don't blow up. Where we set our minds during our daily activities makes a big difference in our responses and reactions when negative circumstances pop up.[17]

---

[17] See the blog on this event at www.barbaramoon.wordpress.com *Grace for Muddy Carpets*

Application: What do you find yourself setting your mind on? Is it mostly negative? Or mostly positive? Begin to catch yourself and turn your thoughts to things of God. Focus on Him. Notice if you see a difference in your reactions according to what you have been thinking about.

"And those who are in the flesh cannot please God. However you are not in the flesh but in the Spirit, if indeed the Spirit of God dwells in you. But if anyone does not have the Spirit of Christ, he does not belong to Him." Romans 8: 8-9

We looked at Romans 8: 5-6 focusing on the words "according" and "setting your mind." Now it will be helpful to look more closely at the word "in" here in verses 8 and 9 and contrast "in" with the word "according." Many have used these verses as a weapon to say that it is very difficult to please God and others have even used them to judge someone's salvation. If we look more closely we will see that here, "in" is about a person who is not a Christian. The determining factor about salvation is whether or not one is "in the Spirit." Does the Spirit dwell in you? If so, you belong to Him, are in Him and you are not "in the flesh." But we can *act* "according to the flesh" if we focus on the material world, our circumstances and try to live in self-effort. There is a difference.

"In" has to do with our state of being; "according" has to do with our actions. For example, a Christian, someone "in the Spirit," might commit the sin of lying. He or she would be walking according to the flesh—trying to stay out of trouble by lying. On the other hand a non-Christian, someone not in the Spirit but in the flesh, might sin by telling a lie, and he or she would also be walking according to the flesh. An observer at that given moment cannot judge whether a person is a Christian or not by looking at their behavior. Behavior does not determine whether a person is a Christian. Sinful actions may appear to be the same in both people, but the question of salvation is whether they are "in the Spirit" or "in the flesh."

Remember that salvation is eternally secure because a new birth has taken place, not because we act a certain way. There are times when all of us want to question a person's salvation because of their behavior. Only God knows, so it's best for us to pray for another person rather than judging and condemning them based on their behavior. Our love and acceptance will take them further down a path to better behavior than will our judging.

> ***Application:*** Is there someone in your life for whom you need to pray rather than judge? Allow Jesus to love them through you as you pray that they will come to know Him.

"Therefore if any man is in Christ, he is a new creature; the old things passed away; behold new things have come." 2 Corinthians 5:17

As we looked at earlier, after being crucified with Christ, something new about us is raised up and seated with Him above. The old is gone and new things have come. This is a glorious truth upon which we want to focus and take deep into our hearts. It is one of the principle pathways to intimacy with Christ, because we no longer have to focus on all the bad things we have done or live out of the condemnation that permeates our society and makes us hate ourselves. It is vital that we learn to separate personhood and behavior so that we can live from how God sees us. (See devotion on Romans 6: 3-4 for more on our personhood and devotion Romans 6:11 for more on separating the two.)

Years ago while on a retreat, as I was reading the book *Birthright: Christian Do You Know Who You Are* by David Needham, God showed me more deeply what it means to be a new creature. It means that those of us who have received Jesus truly are a new creation. When we received Christ, something new was created, not just added. I had been taught that Jesus was added to my life while the "bad me" remained there. Coupled with other things I was learning, Mr. Needham's statements cleared my mind completely to understand that a creation was something that God made out of something that never was there before! A product is made out of things that already exist, but creations are made out of "no things." (Romans 4:17; Hebrews 11:3) To create is to bring into existence. The old person is gone and now we are new, joined to Christ as a new creation.[18]

Although we are new creations we still have emotional wounds that need healing, old ways of thinking, and old beliefs. Walking in intimacy along our journey of faith with God is how we grow, heal and change the old ways, but the spiritual part of us is in essence a new creation. He made something new. When we are tempted to say that it's not true, it will most likely be because we are looking at behavior or appearances. We have most likely lost our peace.

Remember the "Gentle and Quiet Spirit" devotion, 1 Peter 3: 4, where we looked at differences in who we are and what we do? We asked the question, "If I bark, does that make me a dog?" Since we live out of what we believe at the moment, it seems important to notice what we are believing when we lose our peace. Colossians 3: 15 says, "Let the peace of Christ rule in your hearts. . ." God peace is like a sentinel or a referee that tells us how we are doing. When peace is not ruling our hearts, we've lost our peace because something needs to be healed or we're believing a lie from our past or from the enemy. Lost peace is a signal to turn to Jesus and find out what He wants us to know. It always helps to remind ourselves that we are a new creation in Christ. He will show us what needs to be healed or changed when we turn to Him. (We will look at how to tell the truth from a lie in the chapter on Feelings and Appearances.)

---

[18] *Birthright: Christian Do You Know Who You Are*, pages 62-63

> ***Application:*** Do you know that you are a new creation, made new by God? Do you realize when you lose your peace? What do you usually do when that happens? When you lose your peace, turn to Jesus and ask Him what He wants you to know.

"Moreover I will give you a new heart and put a new spirit within you; I will remove the heart of stone from your flesh and give you a heart of flesh. And I will put my Spirit within you and cause you to walk in My statutes, and you will be careful to observe My ordinances." Ezekiel 36:26-27

We have been looking at several verses from the New Testament that indicate the new life we have in Christ. Here we can see God's promise for a new covenant made to Israel during Ezekiel's time. Scholars agree that these promises of a new covenant were prophecies about the coming of Christ. God's people would have a new heart and a new spirit, and God's Spirit would be in them where He would keep the commandments in and through them. We today are on the other side of those promises. Because of Jesus' work on the Cross, we have been made new. Let's look at an illustration that will help us see the depth of this promise from Ezekiel:

> Before receiving Christ we are not connected to God, we cannot go to Heaven. We have a heart of stone. Picture a clear glass filled with Coke. That is the heart of stone—hard and dirty, dead to God. Now, instead of seeing clear, clean water poured into the glass as many have taught, picture the hand of God picking up the glass and instead of just pouring out the Coke and adding water to it—He throws away the glass and replaces it with another cup that is filled with clear, clean water. That is what this verse is saying. We have a new heart—our spirits joined to the Holy Spirit.

The new heart is soft and pliable desiring to walk with God and keep His word.

God has made His prophecies come true in Jesus. All who receive Him as Savior will have a new heart, a new spirit and the God of the Universe living in them.

> ***Application:*** Were you taught that "the bad you" and Jesus both reside in your heart? Think on God's promise in Ezekiel and experience the depth of having a new heart, a new spirit, and being filled with the Spirit. If you have received Jesus, you have a soft, new heart that is joined to Him.

"He who has joined himself to the Lord is one spirit with Him." 1 Corinthians 6:17

Because of what He did on the Cross, Jesus did more than save us from sin and make us a new creation—He actually joined Himself to us. We are one with Him. There is no separation between us. Living in "no separation" is a life-changing way to live. The opposite—separation—is defeating and exhausting. When we live as if Jesus were up in Heaven while we are down here on Earth, we struggle and strive to make things true that are already true. We try to get love through relationships with others, through accomplishments and success, and through material goods, when the truth is, we are already loved, we are complete and provided for. We try to change our bad habits in our own strength when Jesus has said we have to let Him live the Christian life. We carry burdens and worry that we have to fix things and make things happen when Jesus tells us to rest. Being joined to the Lord as one is a mystery and difficult to put into words. You may ask, "How I can be one with Him and still be 'me?'" Let's look at an example from one of my mentors, Laurie Hills:

Picture your hands with one hand palm forward and the back of the other hand, as a fist, in your palm. The fisted hand can turn in towards the fist (Christ) or out to the world when drawn away by temptation or pain that causes us to forget who we are, but the fist is still inside the hand.

Laurie's hand and fist illustration is part of what we have already looked at in the question, "Why do I still sin?" (See "Alive to God" devotion, Romans 6:11 for more on this question.) When we turn away from the union with Christ and focus on the flesh or the world, there is no condemnation. We need only to confess our failure and turn back in to the Spirit.

Application: Being one with the Lord is a foundational truth that will change your life in many ways.[19] Consider this great truth that you are one with the God of the universe, that He loves you so much that He is joined to you. Don't give up until you know it for yourself.

"When He (the Holy Spirit) comes, He will convict you of sin, righteousness and judgment." John 16:8

We have looked at various ways and reasons that we still sin after becoming one with Jesus. For example, we lie to protect ourselves from correction or consequences. We act differently with different people in order to feel accepted. We cheat on our taxes because we don't trust God as our provider. As these examples show us, the principle reason we sin is

---

[19] For more details about our union with Christ, see Dan Stone & Greg Smith, *The Rest of the Gospel, When the partial Gospel has worn you out*, One Press, Dallas, TX

© 2013 Barbara Moon

because we are believing some lie about God, ourselves, our circumstances, or others. Wrong beliefs bring wrong behavior. Unhealed emotions trip us up. We need joy-filled relationships to help us heal and grow.

Sometimes we sin because of lies, but sometimes we believe we are terrible sinners because we have been taught to focus on sin. Leaders and pastors have emphasized sin until we feel like we sin all the time. In his book, *Turkeys and Eagles*, Peter Lord talks about asking people how many times they sin per day. Most people give an answer in the 100's, thinking that sinning numerous times a day is normal. If we think it's normal to sin all the time, we will expect to sin.[20] Our focus will be on sin instead of Jesus and how He has made us righteous. We will even mistake condemnation for conviction of sin. Condemnation says *we* are bad. Conviction of sin says what *we did* was bad.

This verse in John tells us that the Spirit will not only convict us of sin, He will also convict us of our righteousness. That kind of conviction is not often talked about, but it's something we can ask Jesus to do and He will. As we study and take in all these truths about who we are in Christ—that we are holy, righteous, accepted, complete and loved—the Holy Spirit will convict us of our righteousness; He will reveal it to our hearts. When we know we are not "sinners saved by grace," but loved, accepted, precious sons and daughters of God, united to Him with no separation, the intimacy we seek will become reality. Grace and union bring intimacy because we do not have to hold ourselves aloof from a god who is out to get us because of our guilt and sin—we are one with the God who loves us more than we can ever know.

Application: Allow Jesus to convict of you of your righteousness and turn your focus from sin to Him and to His righteousness which is now yours. (II Corinthians 5:21)

---

[20] Peter Lord, *Turkeys and Eagles*, The Seed Sowers, PO Box 3317, Jacksonville, FL 32206, page 78

"*I* am the light of the world; he who follows Me shall not walk in the darkness, but shall have the light of life." John 8:12

"*You* are the light of the world. . ." Matthew 5:14

We see here that Jesus is the light of the world—but so are we. Both of us being light shows us another picture of our union with Jesus: He is the light—and we are the light because we are one. Here is visual that will help you see this truth:

> Picture a candleholder that is made of three parts, just as we are, spirit, soul and body. There is the candleholder itself, (our body) which is sometimes plain, sometimes beautiful, sometimes ordinary, sometimes even ornate. Then there is the candle (our soul). The candle (our soul) sits inside the candleholder (our body). Each candleholder is different. Each candle is different. But there is one thing that is the same—the flame. The light is Jesus in union with our human spirit (the wick). When He shines through us—the candleholders—the light looks different—glowing and flickering through each holder in a unique way. We can see this in a room full of lit candles. The holders can be different colors, shapes, and designs, flickering in different shapes and making various shadows. But the flame is the same.

This is a picture of how Jesus looks when living through us. He looks like the uniqueness of each one of us, diverse and different, while at the same time He will be like Himself, as we know Him and His characteristics from the Bible. Living through us will not only look like what we call spiritual things such as praying, witnessing, preaching and Bible reading. Jesus will live through us when we are washing dishes, changing diapers, working in our offices, playing together, going to school and any other activities we do. Secular and spiritual are the same to those who know union with Christ.

Picturing the candleholders brought me closer to a place of rest and self-acceptance, and made it easier to accept others. I realized that Jesus would look different through each person's unique personality and body and that there was not anything wrong with me or others if we did not fit into some pre-conceived idea of what *He* should look like while living through us. No body-type or personality is better or worse than another. When the flame is lit, (and it never goes out by the way) He is living— living as us. The eternal flame made by Jesus in union with my unique candle sounds to me like the two, Jesus and I, are one.[21]

> ***Application:*** Is there anything about your "candleholder" or your "candle" that you are rejecting? Jesus made them for His glory and loves you just as you are. Talk to Him about your body and your personality. See how He wants to use you, to live through you, to love others, and to serve Him uniquely as no one else can. Let Him shine through your life and light up your world.

"For they disciplined us for a short time as seemed best to them, but He disciplines us for our good, that we may share His holiness. All discipline for the moment seems not to be joyful, but sorrowful; yet to those who have been trained by it, afterwards it yields the peaceful fruit of righteousness." Hebrews 12: 10-11

---

[21] From Barbara Moon, *Leader's Guide to The Rest of the Gospel,* amazon.com, page 24

As we grow in understanding all that God has done through His Son to make us new, sometimes it's difficult to separate who we are from what we do and what it is that needs changing, and what it is that we claim by faith as already true about us. This illustration comes from my second son, Bob Moon, who was just a teenager when we were learning these truths and his youthful zeal, teachability, and faith helped me all the time! What a joy to see a young and uncluttered life be able to explain things of the Lord. His version of growing and changing, though we are already perfect in our spirit, goes something like this.

> Our soul is like a dented tube. The dents are negatives, qualities, habits, etc., that are part of our lives that don't match how God would like us to appear or act. Inside the tube is Jesus, in union with us. It's His job to take care of the dents. He will punch out the dents when and as *He* sees fit. Sometimes we can help and other times we cannot, but we can always co-operate. It's up to Him which dents get "worked on," and when. As we notice other people's dents, we don't try to un-dent them or tell Jesus when and what to do with them. He accepts us with our dents and we accept others with their dents, waiting and co-operating as He fixes dents in His time, speaking to others only as He leads. We can pray for others' dents, but love them where they are, just as Jesus loves us where we are.[22]

God teaches us and grows us through the whole journey of our lives; sometimes using discipline the same as good parents discipline their children. That we need discipline in order to grow does not diminish the fact that in Christ we are complete, accepted, loved and holy. These are true of the inner man. When we live by our old belief systems and old habits we will sin. We have to take responsibility for those sins. Old painful wounds from the past can cause us to behave badly, opposite of who God says we are. We have to take responsibility for those actions, and often pay consequences as well. But in taking responsibility for sin, we do not sin further by beating up on ourselves.

---

[22] *Jewels for My Journey*, page 40

Knowing God's love through Christ's work on the Cross that makes us a new creation changes our growth journey and our perspective on discipline. We will not view God's hand as punishment. When we own our sin, we confess our sins, repent of living in the old ways, and we find healing for our painful memories that keep us stuck. During consequences, we keep our eyes on Jesus, continuing to trust Him and grow intimacy. We will need others to help us make new habits and keep us accountable. We will need Jesus to tell us the truth about the lies we believed. God supplies the power for us when we do our part of repenting, seeking help, studying, and living by faith. These are some of the ways we grow and change. Self-effort won't get us there; neither will self-condemnation and false guilt.

> ***Application:*** Is there anyone in your life whose "dents" you are trying to un-dent? Are you trying to get God to work on yours or another's dents in your timetable? Look to Jesus to know your acceptance and theirs and leave the renewing of the soul to Him.

The LORD your God is in your midst, A victorious warrior. He will exult over you with joy, He will be quiet in His love, He will rejoice over you with shouts of joy." Zephaniah 3:17

In this verse, Zephaniah tells us of God's great love, grace and intimacy. Several years ago, during my divorce I was struggling to believe that I was a new creation, that I was loved and accepted and not alone. It had even become difficult for me to go to church, a feeling I'd never experienced. Finally I began to go back occasionally and one Sunday God gave me a short respite from the pain by showing me again how He sees us in Christ. The draw to get me back to church was a newborn granddaughter, Elysia, whom I got to hold while my daughter-in-law, Elizabeth, did worship team. Every week it felt so good to hold Elysia and just enjoy looking at her. Cuddling her warm body, smelling her baby smell and seeing her precious smiles brought joy to my aching heart. She could not perform in any way and she could not do anything except just be herself. She was delightful to behold.

That Sunday, as I sat there holding Elysia and enjoying who she was, Jesus whispered softly in my heart, *"This is how you are to Me. I enjoy and delight in being with you—in you just being yourself. Even though you're hurting, you're loved and accepted by Me. I am hurting with you."*

Pondering that Jesus loves us, delights in us, and rejoices over us with great joy lessens hurts and builds strength to believe the truth that we are valuable and loved. Knowing we do not have to perform to get His love frees us to rest and be who He made us to be.

Application: Do you know how much Jesus loves and delights in you? Do you realize the freedom from having to perform for acceptance in the same way a baby doesn't have to perform? If not, find a person who does who can help you as you ponder these truths in your heart.

"And go to the exiles, to the sons of your people, and speak to them and tell them, whether they listen or not, 'Thus says the Lord God.'" Ezekiel 4:11

Recently I took a slightly different look at grace as God continued to free me from old habits of co-dependency—the art of making decisions based on what other people will think. In this verse, God is telling Ezekiel that he has to go speak to the people who are stubborn and obstinate. The following is from the blog I wrote on the subject when I took a different look at grace:

A Look at Grace

In the years I studied and learned about grace and union, I gained freedom and understanding of who God says I am in Christ, but grace and union didn't free me completely from a life mired in co-dependency. Along with God, Dr. Jim Wilder was my guide through that life-sucking swamp. When I first began to talk to Dr. Wilder, he told me to go do a word study on the word "nice," I laughed out loud. I immediately knew that word was not in the Bible. I stopped using it and replaced it with the word "kind," but until lately I have to confess I still have allowed that word "nice" too much control over my thinking. Being nice is the number one value in the United States and it's very hard to get past the training we've had about being nice, especially if reared in the South.

As I've struggled through Nice Swamp, trying to get free from the tentacles of fear that sometimes keep me from standing up for what is right, I've often mixed up nice and grace. I want to share a look at grace that is beginning to slice through some of the weeds around my heart.

Freedom is not freedom when I care more about what others will do or say back to me than I do to speak what God says to speak—when He says to speak. Speaking what God wants someone to hear is not being unkind (though they may hear it that way). We speak so they can live. This is what I received from Dr. Wilder's wisdom that helped bring me more balance about grace:

> *God is gracious, but grace does not mean overlooking that which is evil. Grace means dealing with that which is evil. It's not grace to let someone get away with evil while thinking it's good. That is not graciousness; that is foolishness.*

> *Graciousness is confronting a person with the evil that he or she is doing so that they may have a chance to understand what God actually wants and then repent. However because it isn't nice, it's confrontive and not what the person wants to hear, we tend to think that it's not gracious. We think of gracious as just something that makes someone comfortable*

all the time. **Grace does not always make us comfortable—grace saves our life!** *Grace is God giving us the things we need for life, not the things we need to be comfortable. This is a very important distinction.*[23]

I love that phrase in bold: **Grace does not always make us comfortable—grace saves our life!** This was the key phrase that opened my eyes to a fresh look at grace. I clearly understood it concerning salvation and when I was parenting. Jesus was not comfortable when He was saving our lives; I was not comfortable when I loved my children too much to let them misbehave. But I must confess that through the years I've leaned towards ignoring things that I might need to say to someone when my motive was more from fear than from grace. I know it would take an entire book to explore all the facets of when to speak and when to overlook, but for now I'm considering the fear that keeps us from standing up and speaking to someone who is hurting us or others. My desire is to grow in God's inner strength that will stop my wandering in Nice Swamp when I need to be bold and brave. I'm not sure yet how it will look or how it will feel, but I do know it's hard and scary. I want to have what I need for life, real Life, and I want to see giving grace as something that doesn't always make us comfortable. Along with musing on this look at grace, I'm pursuing any wounds that need healing so that fear will not keep me "nice." Jesus in me is kind—but He is also brave.[24]

Application: Do you know the balance of grace for acceptance and grace that does not keep someone comfortable? Do you sometimes overlook things that should be spoken to? Is there a person with whom you need to speak and work out a problem? Ask God to show you when and how. Ask Him to be your courage.

---

[23]More on Dr. Wilder's talk on Ezekiel From Munchie #24, www.lifemodel.org Shepherd's House, Inc. Pasadena, CA

[24] See whole blog at www.barbaramoon.wordpress.com *A Look at Grace*

"As you therefore have received Christ Jesus the Lord, so walk in Him." Colossians 2:6

Paul reminds us to *walk* in Christ Jesus the same way we received Him—by faith. The Holy Spirit wants to reveal to you who you are in Christ. In order to receive the Holy Spirit's revelation of the truth into your heart, you will have to "take it by faith, until it takes you." Seeing yourself as God sees you—a new creation, in union with His Son, Jesus—is life-changing.

Take these verses and think on them as your intimacy with Christ grows and grows. As you realize more and understand better what happened on the Cross, you will find a new sense of yourself that fits the way God intends. Freedom from self-condemnation will encourage you to reach the potential He made you to reach. Trusting God and His truth is the foundation for experiencing all that brings you the intimacy for which you long.

INTIMACY BY FREEDOM FROM THE LAW—RECONCILING GOOD & BAD

"There is therefore, no condemnation for those who are in Christ Jesus. For the law of the Spirit of life in Christ Jesus has set you free from the law of sin and death." Romans 8:1

As we continue to seek intimacy with Jesus, it's vital to understand how He views us in all our messes, failures and struggles. Refusing to take condemnation opens the door widely to know and be known. We could have learned to take condemnation from people in our lives who saw us as bad or communicated to us that we are bad. We could have felt condemnation from the ways we were disciplined as a child. We could have received condemning messages because of mistakes and failures that happened in our lives. These kinds of condemning messages were never true, but as children, our hearts believed what we were told. Dr. Wilder helped me see how these messages work:

> There is no part of ourselves we can see, good or bad about ourselves, without another person. What we need is to be the sparkle in someone's eye. We need comfort and validation for our pains and failures. When we do not get what we need, Satan has his way. Why? That's his standard warfare. He does not want us to get what we need because getting it will directly help us—and the Body of Christ. We will reach our full potential and fulfill the purpose God has planned for us. With those we will soar and dance. That would be the opposite of what the enemy wants for us. He would want for us to keep believing we are bad.[25]

Unlike the enemy, Jesus never condemns us—but He does convict. Condemnation is about our personhood, who we are. Condemning

---

[25] *Jewels for My Journey*, paraphrased from page 170

messages, whether verbal or implied sound like, "You're bad, you never do anything right, you're a failure, a loser, stupid, sinful, inadequate, unloved." The truth about us now in Christ is that we are holy, righteous, blameless, accepted, complete and loved. Unlike condemnation, conviction is about our behavior—which may stink. Stinky behavior must be spoken to and corrected. When God convicts us, or we confront others' behavior without condemnation, it sounds more like, "What you did was wrong; this needs to be corrected; let me help you find another way." Earlier we called that discipline. (Devotion on Hebrews 12:11 in Grace and Union.) Condemnation says you are bad. Conviction says what you did, thought or said is bad. There is a huge difference.

In his lectures and books, Dr. Bill Gillham gives a clear example of the difference: "If our child lies we have a choice to correct them two different ways. We can say, 'You are a liar and we won't have any liars in our house.' Or we can say, 'You lied and we won't have lying in our house.'"[26] These two messages are very different.

> ***Application:*** When you understand the difference in condemnation and conviction, and begin to take the truths about who you are in Christ, you will be free—to take correction when needed, and to not take shame or humiliation when condemnation comes your way. As you go through your day, notice which way you are speaking to others—do you attack their personhood or speak to behavior?

"For what the Law could not do, weak as it was through the flesh, God did, sending His own Son in the likeness of sinful flesh

---

[26] *Lifetime Guarantee*, Harvest House Publishers, Eugene, OR 97402, 1993, pages 44-45

and as an offering for sin, He condemned sin in the flesh, in order that the requirement of the Law might be fulfilled in us, who do not walk according to the flesh, but according to the Spirit." Romans 8: 3-4

"For Christ is the end of the law for righteousness to every one who believes." Romans 10:4

Thanks be to God that we do not have to keep the Law in our own strength. Jesus died to set us free from the Law and now, sets us free on a daily basis as we walk the journey; He is the Law Keeper in our hearts. Each day, moment by moment, we have the choice to walk according to the flesh or to the Spirit. We looked at this concept in the Chapter on Grace and Union, devotion Romans 8:5-6. If we follow the flesh, (*sark* in Greek), we will follow the lies that others have planted in our belief system; we will live in our old habits and try to get our needs met for love and acceptance through other people, through achievements, through money, through food, through popularity.

I remember when Jesus showed me two of the ways that I got my needs met outside of Christ. My bent was towards staying busy and trying to do everything right. It was easy for me to accomplish most anything I set out to do. Two things happened that shook my foundation built on busyness and/or perfectionism. While we were living in Washington, D. C., I had a co-worker who continually criticized everything I did. I literally could not do anything right, from the clothes I wore to the way I conducted meetings. Eventually, I became a depressed mess because no matter how hard I tried, I could not measure up. God used that time in my life to show me how I was looking to others besides Him to tell me if I was accepted and okay. He wanted to work in that area of my life so that I could learn to get my acceptance and worth from Him. Getting needs met outside of Christ is exhausting because we are trying to gain acceptance by performing perfectly. We are trying to keep the Law in our own efforts, through the flesh, instead of seeing ourselves as God does.

The other event took place after we moved to Georgia. I was used to being very busy with children, ministry, studying, and meeting with women to mentor them. After I had the house unpacked and straight, I found myself very bored. There had not been enough time for me to develop relationships, I was not needed in the ministry, and the children were all in school. This was about the time I was learning these truths about where to find my acceptance. Jesus showed me that busyness was one of the ways that I met my own needs in order to feel good about myself. Busyness was also a distraction that kept me from facing uncomfortable circumstances. I repented of that and asked Him to teach me differently. Eventually I learned to rest and wait on the Lord.

Over the years as we learn to follow the Spirit, we will wonderfully experience our acceptance and love needs met through Jesus. We will find it easier to obey because He is living His life through us and keeping the Law in us. We will not *want* to lie, steal, or gossip. If we do sin, we will be bothered greatly. When we hear a "commandment" in our heart from Him, such as, "love that person there who may be difficult to love," we will turn to Jesus and allow Him to love through us. When we feel impatient, we can say, "Thank You, You are my patience here." When we feel anxious, we can say, "You are my peace." (Ephesians 2:14a) For certain, we will still have trials and struggles, but we'll know that we cannot, in and of ourselves, live the Christian life. Only Jesus can, and He wants to live His life through us, as us.

Application: Do you know what you may be using or doing to belong, to feel accepted, worthy or important? Is it perfectionism, food, material things, activities, what other people think? Consider these truths about Christ loving and accepting you and keeping the Law in you. You are free from performing for acceptance.

"Are you so foolish? Having begun by the Spirit are you now being perfected by the flesh? Does He then who provides you with the Spirit and works miracles among you, do it by the works of the Law or by hearing with faith?" Galatians 3: 3 and 5

It's so easy to forget that we were saved by grace through faith and then turn around and try to live by the flesh—our own efforts and our own understanding. Many of us begin our life in Christ by the Spirit with great excitement and zeal. We set out to become the best Christian there is. We want to serve Him and repay Him for all He did for us, but along the way the excitement and zeal burn out. Unknown to most of us, we are tired from our efforts to be perfected by works of the Law. The works of the Law—trying to do the do's and not do the don'ts in our own strength—is very tiring and gets us nowhere fast.

When I first surrendered to Christ, I was very careful to do the do's such as Bible reading, prayer, witnessing and acting kindly. Before I learned to walk by faith and the Spirit, I felt guilty if I missed my time for prayer and Bible reading. For me, the don'ts were not as evident because I was not tempted to steal or lie, but I had plenty of private thoughts that I did not want anyone to know about. I was guilty of yelling at my kids. I had tried for years to stop yelling and when I failed I felt guilty. Finally, when I grew in letting Jesus live through me, He gave me a way that helped me stop yelling.

My oldest son, Jim, age 11 at the time, also struggled with anger. I asked his forgiveness for talking harshly, told him I wanted to stop and asked him if we could we help each other. He agreed and we came up with a signal that would prompt the other that he or she was angry and to give it to Jesus. We would scratch the top of our head in front of the other. It did not take me long to stop talking ugly to my children when one of them was keeping me accountable. Trying to change in our own strength, through the flesh is exhausting. When we trust the Spirit, we see a significant change in our lives and it almost seems like a miracle—the changes are real and lasting.

Speaking harshly is an outward sin that everyone can see. For "invisible" sins such as bad attitudes, wrong motives, or hateful thoughts we also walk with Jesus the same way we began with Him as Savior—by faith, allowing Him to live through us. We cannot change these behaviors in our own strength. We have to depend on the Spirit and co-operate with His leadings and convictions. The second we realize we've had a hateful thought or bad attitude, we agree with God that it was wrong, receive forgiveness and seek what *He* would have us do about it. Making resolutions to be carried out by the strength of our wills does not work.

Sometimes we fail to get "perfected by the Spirit" when someone rejects us or condemns us, or we hear old messages in our thoughts that are lies from the past. For example, whenever I blew it, my tendency was to think or say aloud, "I can't do anything right. I'm no good for anything." Then I would beat up on myself in my mind and promptly resolve to try even harder to do everything right next time. I was trying to be "perfected by the flesh" instead of relying on the Spirit. What we need to do is admit that beating up on ourselves is sin, then, by faith, turn to Jesus and take what He says about us, refusing to take those kinds of thoughts or what the world and other people may throw at us. Jesus says we are loved and accepted, complete and adequate in Him. The works of the Law will not perfect us—only God's truth through a relationship with the Spirit can set us free.

I like the way Dr. Bill Gillham told us to look at ourselves after admitting we have sinned: "I am a holy, righteous, blameless, accepted, loved son (daughter) of the King, who sins once in a while, but really doesn't want to."

Application: Do you tend to beat up on yourself when you mess up? Admit your mistake, receive forgiveness, then take what Jesus says and refuse to take condemnation. Do you have someone to keep you accountable as you work on areas of your life? Notice when you are trying to fix yourself in your own strength and turn to Jesus and rely on Him.

"No one is justified before God by the law, for 'The righteous shall live by faith.' But the law is not of faith, rather 'The one who does them shall live by them.'" Galatians 3:11-12 ESV-English Standard Version

Law and faith are opposites. We cannot stand with one foot in the law and one foot in faith. It's an either/or proposition. If the Law could save us, Jesus would not have had to die. (I Corinthians 15:14, 17) But even as a Christian, we cannot keep the Law. Maybe we can keep some of them while other people keep some different ones, but this will not save anyone or help them grow. In this verse, Paul tells us that we can go ahead and try to keep the Law if that suits us, but we better be sure we can live by every single rule. Every single rule includes gossip, ungodly anger, strife, jealousy, coarse jesting, envy. Oh, dear! We can quickly see it's better to live by faith and walk in the Spirit. We can't keep the Law; we need a Savior and His power.

> ***Application:*** Do you find yourself thinking there are "degrees" to sin—that some are worse than others? (See James 2:10) Consider that bad thoughts, bad attitudes, gossip and jealousy are as much a part of the Law as stealing, lying and adultery. Jesus took the Law and made it stronger when He said to love even our enemies and fine-tuned it by saying, "To look on a woman to lust in for her in one's heart was to commit the sin of adultery." (Matthew 5:28) Ask Jesus to show you what you need to see and trust Him to keep the Laws in you.

"But before faith came, we were kept in custody under the law, being shut up to the faith which was later to be revealed. Therefore the Law has become our tutor to lead us to Christ, that we may be justified by faith. But now that faith has come, we are no longer under a tutor." Galatians 3:23-25

Is the Law bad? No! There are other places where Paul, the writer of this verse, says it's holy, righteous and good. (Romans 7: 12 and 16, and 1 Timothy 1:8.) So why did God give the Law? In the New Testament times, a child who was to become an heir had a tutor to train him for his future adulthood tasks. When the child was grown and mature, he no longer needed the tutor. God gave us the Law, because like children we need a tutor to show us what we don't know and what we cannot do ourselves—we need a Savior.

Like the Israelites in the Old Testament, a good example of people trying to keep the Law—a task way too big—we have to learn over and over that we cannot do it on our own. God told His people what He wanted and they would promise to do it—then fail. They promised, started over—and failed—time and time again. They needed a Messiah who would live in them and be the power necessary for them to live God's way. Like the Israelites, we promise in our own strength to stop our pet sins, to change our bad habits or to start new, good ones—and we fail. We cannot keep the Law in our own strength. We have to come to the end of striving and trying.

The Law leads us to Christ, where we have to come by faith, find out we cannot keep the Law, and know we need Jesus both for salvation and living. When we understand what He has done and who we are in Him, we no longer need the Law. We will understand that we don't *want* to sin; we will be less likely to sin; we will no longer be sin-conscious and self-condemning.

Application: Do you realize that if you're a Christian, you don't *want* to sin? Have you been taught that you are a "sinner" and prone to do bad things? Relax and enjoy your freedom to let Christ convict you. He is capable to make it clear—and do it without condemnation.

"It was for freedom that Christ set us free; therefore keep standing firm and do not be subject again to a yoke of slavery." Galatians 5:1

In the picture of freedom we have in the verse above, Paul tells us to keep standing firm through a life of faith and grace. We have been set free. As we look at the verse, some questions arise: What does Paul mean by "a yoke of slavery?" From what did Christ set us free? Paul was writing to the Galatians because some leaders were telling them that they had to keep the Mosaic Law after they received Christ. They had to perform rituals and do the do's and not do the don'ts in order to be acceptable to God. Trying to do that would negate all that Christ had done on the Cross. He died to set us free from the Law. Man cannot keep the rules and regulations in and of himself, and trying to keep them is like having the chains of a slave bound around one's neck.

The people of Paul's time would have had a clear picture of slavery any place they looked. Some to whom he wrote may have been slaves themselves. So the question arises, "What would a yoke of slavery be today? How do we try to "keep the Law?" We looked at modern-day do's and don'ts in the devotion of Galatians 3: 3 and 5 a few pages back. We named some as prayer and Bible reading, witnessing, and serving at church. These activities are meant to be done from a heart full of love, not out of duty under the "law." When the motive is duty and feels like drudgery, we are wearing a yoke of slavery. Other "yokes" could be trying to get people to love us, being afraid to fail, or living in fear. Paul says to stand firm against anything that says we have to perform a certain way in order to be acceptable to God.

Application: Is there something which you feel that have to do in order to be accepted—at home, at church, at play? Are you doing some things out of duty rather than love? Talk to Jesus about these places and allow Him to change your attitudes and beliefs so that you can be free.

"Come to Me, all you who are weary and heavy laden, and I will give you rest. Take My yoke upon you and learn of Me, for I am gentle and humble in heart. And you shall find rest for your souls. For My yoke is easy and My load is light." Matthew 11: 28-30

Trying to get people to love us, being told or feeling like we have to perform rituals and keep whatever modern "laws" that have been perpetuated by Christian groups is very exhausting—that yoke of slavery is heavy. The burden is on us to do outward things in order to get, or keep, God's and other people's acceptance. We call that "living by performance based acceptance—or PBA." In this verse we see that Jesus mentions another yoke; this yoke is His yoke—it's easy and light. Jesus and Paul both agree that we do not have to carry heavy burdens and wear the heavy yoke of trying to keep the Law. PBA is a form of the Law—it makes us weary and heavy laden—and we never feel worthy and valuable because we always fail to get it right.

Trying to perform for acceptance leads to failure because we cannot ever get it all right all the time. Our culture is full of messages that say we are not valuable unless we're rich, thin, smart and beautiful. We must be successful at our career, not be a stay-at-home mom, always be politically correct in our speech, and agree with the world's values. Rejection is the mud thrown in the face of anyone who does not measure up. Because of emotional neglect growing up, we feel unworthy, unloved, and unimportant. In families, children are compared to others, abused for mistakes and expected to be perfect. Jesus' yoke is the opposite of PBA—

it is easy and His burden is light because He is the Other in the yoke with us. He does the work. We do our part, but in His strength and power. The yoke is a relationship. Performing perfectly will not be a burdensome necessity when we learn to walk in the truth of our freedom, in intimacy with Him.

I remember an incident where I had to stand firm in Jesus' yoke. It happened a few months after we joined Campus Crusade and began to live by faith. I was sharing with a relative how difficult it was some days not to know where our income was coming from or when we would get it. My relative valued a steady income and thought we were crazy to be living by faith. The relative remarked, "When is Jim going to get a real job?" That comment hurt because we strongly believed that we were right where God wanted us in spite of it being difficult. I had to stand firm and not be pulled into trying to perform the way someone else wanted me to perform.

Application: Are there any places in your life that you are trying to perform a certain way in order to get acceptance or feel valuable? If so, talk to Jesus about it and take His yoke that is easy. Stand firm in the truth that you do not have to perform perfectly even when your feelings, or another person, tell you otherwise.

"The sting of death is sin, and the power of sin is the law; but thanks be to God who gives us the victory through our Lord Jesus Christ." I Corinthians 15:56-57

I love this verse; it is so true. For many years I did not have a clue what "the power of sin is the law" meant but I surely lived it out. Here is how I lived it out: Picture yourself walking along a beautiful flower-laden path in a lovely park on a warm spring day. As you meander slowly through the park enjoying the flowers, the birds and the squirrels, you spy a park bench that seems to call you to sit for a while. When you walk over to the bench, you realize you will not be able to sit and ponder—there's a sign on the bench that says "WET PAINT-Do Not Touch." But like the verse says, the law arouses sin. When the law says, "Do not," you must. You have to stick out your finger and touch the paint. We all feel that pull when we see, "Do not. . ." That is what this verse means.

Because the Law arouses in us the desire to break it, the Law cannot save us. The Law shows us what is right, but it does not have the power necessary for us to live out what is right. When Jesus died, part of what He did was to set us free from the Law. In Him we already have victory over sin because we have a new life. The Law is still around, but we are free from getting our acceptance by trying to keep all the rules and perform perfectly. We are loved and accepted and free because of Jesus. We exercise faith and rest in Him.

Although the pulls we feel with "do-not-touches" are natural responses, they have no power over us because we now have a supernatural power living in us in the Person of the Holy Spirit. We walk in victory over sin aroused by the Law. When we feel the pull to touch the "wet paint," we can turn to Jesus and rely on His power to walk right past that "bench." If we touch the "wet paint," faith will take us to His forgiveness and reconciliation. (We'll see more about how we're free from the Law in following devotions and more on temptation in the chapter on Rest and Peace, devotion James 1: 14-15.)

Application: Are you getting a picture of how the Law works? It is good, but you cannot keep it yourself. Watch for places and times where you are still under the Law and replace those with freedom to fail, freedom to live, freedom to not perform perfectly. God will not condemn you; He loves you beyond your dreams.

"But I say, 'Walk by the Spirit and you will not carry out the desires of the flesh. For the flesh sets its desire against the Spirit, and the Spirit against the flesh, for these are in opposition to one another, so that you may not do the things that you please. But if you are led by the Spirit, you are not under the Law.'" Galatians 5: 16-18

When I was growing up, the first part of verse 16 was taught in a reversed order. The admonition I was taught was, "Try really hard not to carry out the desire of the flesh and then you will walk in the Spirit." So I tried really hard to keep those laws and rules, whatever they were in the circle I was in. I loved God. I wanted to do right. I wanted to obey. I tried. It did not always work out.

Dan Stone[27] tells a good story that illustrates trying to keep the laws of whatever circle one is in: When Dan was a pastor in Kentucky, it was okay to smoke because the people were tobacco growers. But it was forbidden for young people to swim together—that was a terrible sin. Then Dan moved to Florida to pastor and there it was a terrible sin to smoke. But the young people could go swimming together—water was everywhere. Each congregation was deciding on its own what was right and wrong. This happens many times all over the world.

We as humans do not determine what is right and wrong. When we try to decide, we are walking by the flesh. Before we know that we are freed from the Law, some of us try harder to keep the rules; others stop trying—others never try at all. Here is what I know—the Law will get us every time—it will win—we will fail to keep it. Discovering that Jesus had freed me from all that trying and striving was shouting material. It felt so good! Yes, I might mess up still, but it was a lot better being led by the Spirit who loves me and cleanses me from all sin. (1 John 1:9) He just wants us to agree with Him about our failures and receive the forgiveness that is

---

[27] Dan was a personal friend who came often to speak to our home church. His tapes have been made into a book and where I can give the page number I will. If there is no page number, I remember the story from personally hearing it. *The Rest of the Gospel-When the partial Gospel has worn you out,* by Dan Stone & Greg Smith, One Press, Dallas, TX, 2000

already there. (1 John 1:9, Ephesians 1:7) There is no longer a place for condemnation and false guilt. (Romans 8:1)

Application: As you go about your week begin to take note of places that you are trying to be "spiritual" by *not* following rules of the flesh instead of living by the Spirit. Put this verse in the correct order. When you get frustrated with man's rules do you usually stop trying, or try harder? How do you need to rely on Jesus to live through you? Watch for times you take condemnation and false guilt so that you can get free from following the flesh and gain intimacy with Christ through the Spirit.

"You shall not surely die! For God knows that in the day you eat from it your eyes will be opened, and you will be like God, knowing good and evil." Genesis 3:4-5

When we "walk by the Spirit" there is no longer a place for condemnation and false guilt Condemnation and false guilt are part of the flesh. The flesh is part of the consequences that came from Adam and Eve eating the fruit of the tree of the knowledge of good and evil. God told Adam and Eve not to eat of the fruit of that tree or they would surely die. Satan in the form of a serpent came to Eve and told her to eat it, that it would be good. Eve ate and so did Adam. In that moment they lost their innocence and relationship with God. They died spiritually and later would die physically. As a result of those losses from eating the fruit, we humans believe we can decide what is good and bad; we lean on our own understanding instead of listening to God. (Proverbs 3: 5)

Living by our own understanding and trying to get our needs met outside of Christ is a good definition of "flesh." Many of us live from lies that the flesh tells us. Here are some examples: If we have to confront someone with a problem and it hurts their feelings, the flesh says, "If someone hurts, then I'm bad." Or if we try to fix a problem or love someone who doesn't receive the love, the flesh says, "If something doesn't work out, then I'm wrong. I need for things to be the way I want, so I will feel good about myself—loved and accepted."

Application: Do you have the lie in your mind that you are bad if someone hurts or you're not loved if things don't work out? Begin to notice the times that you are trying to figure out what is good and bad so that you can end those lies and experience freedom.

"But if you are led by the Spirit you are not under the Law . . ." Galatians 5: 18

Jesus came to reveal truth and teach us a new way to live, not to make things look right according to rules. Let's look at some places in Scripture where God's truth collided with the Law. Remember when Jesus healed the lame man beside the pool on the Sabbath? And the time He healed a man's withered hand right in the synagogue?[28] The Pharisees, those leaders who lived by the Law, got very upset with Jesus because He broke the Law as they interpreted it—"But the seventh day is a Sabbath of the Lord your God: in it you shall not do any work. . . " (Exodus 20: 10). The Pharisees were blind to who Jesus was, and to His compassion for the sick, because they were so focused on the rules that they had added to God's commandments.

In these instances, we can see that the Pharisees focused on how to obey the Law, but missed having a heart of compassion; while Jesus seemed to break the Law, but acted on His heart of compassion. We face

---

[28] John 5: 1-17; Matthew 12: 9-14

situations like these sometimes, and it becomes hard to find the right path to walk. We want to understand the difference between being "led by the Spirit" and being "under the Law." This difference became clearer for me as I struggled to walk along a very different path for my life than the path I'd imagined.

After exhausting many avenues of biblical counseling in our marriage, it became evident that my marriage would not survive. I had grown up with the desire to stay married to my husband for my whole life. When it became clear that this was not going to be, I was broken hearted. People gave me all kinds of advice during this time, and as I was trying to understand how to walk this out, Dr. Wilder helped me learn how *not* to be "under the Law" but be "led by the Spirit."

Divorce is a very sticky and complex situation and our culture's views on divorce have changed drastically. It's very difficult to look at what Scripture says and at the same time to understand what people are going through behind closed doors. It's not my purpose here to open a debate about divorce; my purpose is to encourage you to learn to hear the Spirit's voice and not lean on rules—a difficult concept that needs the Spirit's revelation. When we live under the Law, we can just about go crazy trying to figure things out.

On one hand God says He hates divorce, and on the other hand Ezra tells the Israelites to divorce their pagan wives. And then we read what Moses and Jesus said.[29] These seem to be contradictory teachings about divorce in the Bible. Focusing on them causes us to go back and forth in our minds without really listening to the Spirit. That's how it feels to be under the Law and be trying to figure out what to do on our own.

While going through my divorce, I had no boxes in which to put my thinking. If I tried to figure it out on my own, my emotions brought chaos and fear. I knew these verses about following the Spirit and not the Law, but it was not easy to walk them out, because Christians are not supposed to divorce. Divorce is often viewed as an unforgiveable sin and so many people get hurt. I had to learn to cling to Jesus by praying and listening to His voice instead of listening to my fretting mind that could not figure out

---

[29] Malachi 2: 16; Ezra 10:3; Deuteronomy 24:1-3 and Matthew 5:31.

how to go through this situation. I reminded myself that Jesus knows how much it hurts to be misunderstood and rejected; He does not condemn and He acts from His heart of compassion. I knew His voice fairly well and I spent much time conversing with Him about all the aspects of what was going on. I took nothing lightly. It was a very painful time but the entire process brought more intimacy with Jesus as I spent lots of time seeking Him in prayer and asking for His guidance. I had to trust His voice even when it seemed to be leading me contrary to what the rules said. I know that marriages can be saved if both people work on it; I've seen it happen, and rejoiced when couples who were far apart were able to come back together. But I also know that this is not always the case.

In spite of the divorce, as I've mentioned before, through listening to the Spirit, our family has worked through much of the pain and healed enough to be able to be together at holidays and birthdays with relationships that are loving and kind. Divorce is not an unforgiveable sin and does not have to be the end of the world. Jesus focused on people, their needs and their hurts, not on do's and don'ts. When these types of hard situations are in the picture, I believe that's our calling as well.

Application: Do you know someone who is going through a hard situation like divorce? They need your love more than your advice. The pain is horrendous regardless of the circumstances and reasons. Ask Jesus how you can best help. If you are the person, pray diligently about the situation and listen for His guidance. Don't take condemnation.

". . . walk by the Spirit and you will not carry out the desires of the flesh." Galatians 5:16

". . . speaking the truth in love, we are to grow up in all aspects into Him who is the head, even Christ." Ephesians 4:15

Learning to walk by the Spirit takes practice and courage. When we need to speak to someone who has hurt us there is room for much misunderstanding. Dr. Wilder talked to me about those times when we need to tell someone who is not very mature that they have hurt us. At those times, it's easy to get defensive and angry over hurt feelings. They may accuse, blame or attack; it's easy to dread their reaction to what we say and back down from a confrontation out of fear. We need to say, "ouch" when we're hurt, but we will have to pray about what to say, how to say it and when to say it, considering that the person may misunderstand. Usually when we tell an immature, wounded person that they hurt us, they interpret our message as saying "you are bad," "you are messed up" and "you lack value" instead of just hearing us saying, "ouch." What we're trying to say is more like, "I'm hurting because when you did _____, I felt _____." Or, "When you do _____, it hurts because _____." We want to separate their behavior from their personhood.

These kinds of confrontations are difficult because there's often an unconscious rule in some people's thinking that says, "If I'm getting corrected, then I'm not valuable." When the flesh is giving these kinds of messages and interpreting them as attacks to our personhood, it's easy for everyone to become defensive instead of working through a problem. When led by the Spirit, we will be able to anticipate those messages that come to their mind saying they are bad and lack value. After prayerfully considering that God is telling us to speak, we can preface our confrontation by assuring the person that what we are going to say is not about their value. We want to talk in order to work things out so we can have a better relationship. Hopefully if we stay calm and speak kindly it will be easier to avoid getting defensive and along the way they will learn that "ouches" are not bad.

Application: Is there anyone in your life to whom you need to say, "ouch?" Pray about how and when to talk to them. Let the reason you talk to be so that you may have a better relationship with each other.

"He who trusts in his own heart is a fool, But he who walks wisely will be delivered." Proverbs 28: 26

When I was teaching school, I made a decision that turned out badly which resulted in me losing that job. I settled in to bear it the rest of my life. Then I made another decision where the negative consequences led me to beat up on myself some more. Because I was using the negative consequences to decide that what I had done was "bad," I was beating up on myself for how I handled it. We often believe, after a choice we've made, "Whatever happens I have to follow this out." Dr. Wilder reminded me that I was trying to figure out the right thing to do on my own. I was believing, "I have to figure out the right thing to do. Consequences from decisions are irreversible." When experiencing a dilemma, it's easy to forget that there is usually more than one choice in a situation. We need to be led by the Spirit so we're free from the Law and self-condemnation. When we're tempted to say, "Follow that rule no matter what," we reframe it by turning to Jesus and listening to His voice. When we know what Jesus is saying, we obey. Sometimes His voice does not make sense at first; sometimes He leads against what the majority might call "right." Think about how many people broke the Nazi's laws to hide the Jewish people during World War II.

What do we do with a choice we made that turns out looking bad, especially if we took time to consider the choice? Doubts about our choices often bring self-condemnation. Dr. Wilder encouraged me to consider looking at choices from a different perspective. I began to see that instead of worrying about making the right choices and taking condemnation when we fail, it's more important to consider the effects our choices have on others in the world around us. That changes our focus from self to others— from the flesh to the Spirit. How does an attitude of self-condemnation affect others? How does condemning others for their failures affect those around us? When we or others fail, we don't have to go down with the ship. Grace and growth are available; learning from mistakes is valuable. If we don't get grace from those around us, we have to grieve that we didn't get grace, but still follow our heart and what the Spirit is saying. The flesh wants us to beat up on ourselves. As Dr. Wilder told me, "You may have to ride with a skunk, (*pay consequences*) but you do not have to brush its fur (*make things worse by beating up on yourself*)."[30]

Application: As you walk through life and mess up here and there, try not to ruffle the skunk's fur. Instead of beating up on yourself, remember that you are just a dusty, bent arrow who cannot hit the target without the Archer. When you think you've made a wrong decision after praying about it, ask God, "What were *You* shooting at, when I made that decision?"[31] Follow the Spirit and allow Him to show you the effects you have on those around you. Ask Him to make those effects come from His life and His love in the Spirit, and not the flesh.

---

[30] See my blog by this title at www.barbaramoon.wordpress.com

[31] From Dr. Wilder in a phone conversation.

"You search the Scriptures, because you think that in them you have eternal life; and it is these that bear witness of Me, and you are unwilling to come to Me that you may have life." John 5: 39-40

". . . but our adequacy is from God, who also made us adequate as servants of a new covenant, not of the letter, but of the Spirit; for the letter kills, but the Spirit gives life." II Corinthians 3: 5-6

As a Christian, only going by the Bible to try to figure out what to do is a form of living under the Law and does not always work well either. Dr. Wilder helped me see better what Jesus and Paul are saying in these verses that go along with Paul's words about being led by the Spirit and not the flesh. When the flesh looks only at the Law for direction, it tries to determine who is at fault or what should have been done. Again we are trying to pick the right thing to do. What if the "right thing to do" does not line up with what our heart is saying or with what we sense Jesus is saying? Going against our heart will "kill" us inside. The letter of the Law cannot bring life; only the Spirit brings life. When we ignore those pulls from the flesh messages to figure out things on our own, we will follow our Father. Unlike those who self-righteously follow rules, God never asks, "Who is at fault here?" He only asks, "What happened here?" (Genesis 3: 8-13) We are just witnesses. Witnesses don't blame or condemn, they bear witness to Jesus and bring life—to others and to themselves. The Scriptures turn us to Jesus—life is in Him, not rules.

Application: Do you sense that you have a good balance between simply seeing the "rules" of the Scripture and the guidance of the Holy Spirit? Do you ever hurt others because of strictness to rules? Let the Spirit give you a better balance. Seek intimacy with Jesus, not rules.

"It is a trustworthy statement deserving full acceptance, that Christ Jesus came into the world to save sinners, among whom I am foremost of all." 1Timothy 1:15

"To me, the very least of all the saints, this grace was given, to preach to the Gentiles the unfathomable riches of Christ." Ephesians 3:8

As we get close to the end of this chapter, let's take a balanced look at ourselves and our identities. We learned in the chapter on Grace and Union how we can separate personhood and behavior. We know that who we are and what we do are different. So what does Paul, the writer of this verse mean when he writes that he is the foremost of sinners? What does he mean in the Ephesians verse when he says is the least of the saints? Is he a sinner or a saint? Answering this question will help us understand what I call "the good-bad split."

In knowing who we are in Christ, we know that God says we are holy, righteous, blameless, accepted, and loved. In many of his letters Paul addressed his readers as "saints."[32] Yet in the letter he wrote to the people in Corinth we can see that the people were not behaving well at all. Were they saints or sinners? To understand Paul's meaning, and how it applies to us, it helps to distinguish between personhood and behavior.

As Christians we can act according to what God says or we can choose to go against His ways, principles, promises and truths. We can build people up or we can tear them down. We can act humbly or we can act defensively. Because we still live in our earthly bodies, we will sin, but

---

[32] Saints: I Corinthians 1:2 and II Corinthians 1:1; Ephesians 1:1, Philippians 1:1, Colossians 1:2; The Corinthians' behavior: I Corinthians Chapters 5 and 6

God has already provided forgiveness, that when received, will transform our lives. Through the Savior we can experience an abundant life full of intimacy with Him.

After salvation, we can still choose to do wrong things, often because we are believing lies. This does not mean we're against God, but it can make us feel like we're sinners and not saints.[33] It seems from what Paul says here and what we looked at in Grace and Union—we are "saints" who can act like "sinners" when we forget who we are in Christ and make bad choices. Until we get to Heaven, the possibility of always making the right choice is not a reality. There is within us, who know and love God, the possibility to act differently than who He made us to be. When those times happen, knowing we are "saints who sometimes sin" allows us to take our actions back to Jesus without fear. Acknowledging where we went wrong, asking His forgiveness, and accepting the consequences for our actions brings greater intimacy with Him. On the other hand, if we define ourselves by our actions when we mess up, we'll hide in shame instead of running to Him. This inner struggle between who we are and what we do is part of the good/bad split.

Application: Is it your custom to run to Jesus for forgiveness or to hide in shame when you make a bad choice? Consider who you are in Him—a saint who sometimes sins. How will knowing that make a difference in your life?

---

[33] See Chapter on Salvation, devotion "We have eternal security." See Chapter on Grace and Union, "Part Two: The Soul" for more about lies we believe.

"And His disciples asked Him, saying, 'Rabbi, who sinned, this man or his parents, that he should be born blind?' Jesus answered, 'It was neither, that this man sinned nor his parents; but it was in order that the works of God might be displayed in him.'" John 9:2-3

We must come to terms with the "good and bad" within us. The good in us is not in and of ourselves—it comes from the "works of God." The bad behavior we exhibit is from choices we make to believe in left-over lies and from unhealed wounds that cause our feelings to be so strong in the moment that they lead us astray. As we continue to analyze separating personhood and behavior we will find it easier to see ourselves the way God does—saints who can act like sinners. The important issue is not to think, believe, or accept that we are bad just because we act badly, or because bad things happened to us. This is especially true about bad things that happened when we were young which cause us to decide, subconsciously, down deep inside, "I'm bad." Believing "I'm bad because bad things happened to me" cripples our intimacy with Christ. He wants us to see ourselves the way He sees us—in Him—and love ourselves the way He loves us. We will need healing from the bad things that happened.

While getting counseling during my divorce, God finished healing a childhood trauma that was partially healed by knowing who I was in Christ. Sometimes resolving a childhood trauma is like peeling an onion—there are layers. We might touch part of it, but the deepest pain comes up later. Without going into details, let's just say that as a young teen, a person I was dating took advantage of my innocence. Learning my identity in Christ had healed a large portion of this trauma, but the deep down belief, "I'm bad" had not been fully resolved. Add to this the then current situation of going through a divorce in a Christian community, and there was enough good fuel to re-ignite and inflame this message: "I'm bad." During one phone conversation, Dr. Wilder encouraged me to listen only to God about whether I was good or bad. I would have to listen to the Spirit and not listen to anyone around me who communicated that I was bad to be going through a divorce. I would also have to continue working on the deeper issue from my childhood that was feeding the fire about the divorce.

As I worked on the left-over pieces of the trauma, I realized just how deeply a part of me felt unloved and bad. Dr. Wilder encouraged me in this deeper pain to stop rejecting myself because of what had happened. He told me to embrace the part of myself that felt unloved and bad, to love myself right there. When bad things happen to us, what we long for is to be loved, validated and comforted. When we do not get that, the pain is horrendous and we internalize, "I'm bad." If unresolved, we then carry the pain of wanting to be loved by people who did not love us. That's a God-like thing. He wants to be loved by people who don't love Him. He understands. He is with us to validate, comfort and embrace the places that hurt.

When, after bad things happen to us and we decide, "I'm bad," the result is self-rejection. Part of resolving the good/bad split is to get healing from the wounds that make us reject ourselves and then to see that our goodness comes from Christ and what He has done. As we looked at in Grace and Union, not only are our sins forgiven, we have a new life in Christ. That truth has to penetrate all those layers where we have believed, "I'm bad." As we turn to Jesus and recognize He was there with us when the bad things happened, He validates and comforts us, the deep healing comes and we will rest and experience peace without self-rejection.

Perhaps it will help to think of the good/bad split this way: before salvation, everyone *is* "bad" and can *do* either "good or bad" things. (John 8:44, Romans 3:23) After salvation, Christians *are* "good" and can *do* both "good and bad" things. (Ephesians 1:4, I John 1:9)[34] In both conditions, we have to come to grips with the fact that we need Christ. In Christ we are a new creation, but there are characteristics, attitudes, behaviors, beliefs, and thoughts that God needs to change. Just as children around the age of two have to realize that the mother who hugs them is the mother who disciplines them, we who have done, and can do, bad things have to realize we are so valuable that God sent Jesus to save us. Resolving the good/bad split over bad things we have done is easiest accomplished by receiving forgiveness, separating personhood and behavior; getting healing for the

---

[34] Think about a famous person who has done great philanthropic works, but is not a Christian. Good works do not make a person a Christian.

bad things that happened to us is best accomplished by realizing Jesus was there with us and separating personhood and circumstances. In both cases, we must know who we are in Christ and experience His healing presence.

> ***Application:*** If you had bad things happen to you while growing up, get with a good counselor who will help you allow yourself to feel the pain and, in your heart and mind, embrace and love yourself inside until you are healed by Jesus' presence. Let there be no self-rejection that says, "I'm bad" for wanting to be loved, validated and comforted. Let there be no lingering thoughts that it was your fault that something bad happened to you. For more on this issue, see my blog on *Resolving the Good/Bad Split* at www.barbaramoon.wordpress.com

"There is therefore, no condemnation for those who are in Christ Jesus. For the law of the Spirit of life in Christ Jesus has set you free from the law of sin and death." Romans 8:1

Experiencing freedom from condemnation and performance-based living is like having a huge mountain removed from your shoulders. That truth alone can change your life and move you towards intimacy with Christ. As you separate personhood and behavior, you will not fall into the trap that says Christians have two natures fighting inside, and condemnation will fall by the wayside. The battle is not with two natures, the battle is between listening to the flesh or the Spirit. Before Paul knew Jesus, he followed the flesh, persecuting and killing the people who would one day become his brothers and sisters. After Paul learned the depth and breadth of the Gospel, he knew freedom from the flesh and the Law. He knew he was forgiven and embraced the brothers and sisters whom he had persecuted. Because they, too, knew Jesus, they forgave Paul and welcomed him as an apostle.

Like Paul, you are loved no matter what you do and God is waiting and eager to transform any part of your life and behavior in which you will co-operate with Him. He waits for your confession of any sin you do, your honesty to own up to your need for Him, and your humility to follow the Spirit and not try to figure out what is not yours to figure out. He is the power you need and the love that you seek. Intimacy is worth the pain it takes to accept responsibility for our actions, attitudes, healing and growth. Keep the balance.

INTIMACY THROUGH SUFFERING AND TRIALS

"Consider it all joy my brethren, when you encounter various trials, knowing that the testing (proving) of your faith produces endurance, and let endurance have its perfect result that you may be perfect and complete, lacking in nothing." James 1:1 and 2

". . . you have been distressed by various trials, that the proof of your faith, being more precious than gold . . . may be found to result in praise and glory and honor at the revelation of Jesus Christ." I Peter 1: 6 and 7

Trials come in various forms such as trusting God for finances, finding a new job, losing a loved one or life circumstances that lead to feeling as if we're walking in darkness. Joy is not a word that we usually associate with trials, but we can identify with trials testing our faith. James is encouraging us to look at our trials through God's eyes, the only way to joy in them.

When we face trials and suffering, these kinds of crossroads in our journeys can go one of two ways: we can pull back and turn away from God or we can turn and hold on to Him even though we feel like we're in the dark as to what's going on. If we turn to God and cling to him, we will enter that place that will take us deeper in intimacy with Him. That will be where the testing of our faith produces endurance.

Trials—difficulties in our lives—are the very tools that God uses to prove our faith, to show us where we are in our journey with Him and draw us to further intimacy with Him. After a log bridge was built over a gulch in the Old West, the time came for the bridge to be opened. The engineer who had overseen the project would drive the train out onto the bridge and stop. We might think the engineer was very brave to drive out on the odd-looking log structure and stop the train, but in fact, the engineer was not testing the bridge before it opened for use—he was proving what he already knew it would do. In the same way God proves what He knows about us when He uses trials to prove our faith and grow intimacy.

God knows that deep in our hearts, what we truly want and long for is intimacy with Him—and He knows what it takes to get us there. He made us that way. The engineer wants to get trains across a deep gulch and he must follow what it takes to make a bridge. Just as it takes sweat and blood and lots of hard work to build a bridge, intimacy with Jesus develops quite often through trials and painful events such as illnesses, car accidents, divorces, rebellious children and financial losses. It's true that God does sometimes use blessings to develop intimacy with Jesus, using them to draw us to Himself, but it seems to be part of our humanness that we decide to acknowledge and talk to Him more when circumstances are difficult. We must trust God to know whether it will take trials or blessings to grow our intimacy.

Sometimes when painful difficulties come into our lives, instead of acknowledging and talking to God, in our hearts we're angry at Him and we don't believe He wants to be there for us. We might not even want to be with people who know God and could help us. James and Paul are telling us here that we can find joy in our suffering and trials because, when we look to God for comfort and guidance He will turn our sorrow to precious gold—we will grow closer to Him. There is nothing more valuable than intimacy with our God.

As the Engineer of our faith, God already knows how we will stand up during trials and difficulties, the same way the bridge engineer knows that the bridge he's designing will hold up all the cars or trains that will pass over it. Bridge builders follow a set of blueprints, and if we don't have our own set of "spiritual blueprints" we might find ourselves using addictions or denial to combat the stress we feel in difficult circumstances. God Himself is our blueprint. He has given us Jesus and the Scriptures to show us how much He loves us and how He wants us to live. When we talk to Him, listen to Him, and follow His direction even when life is hard, He blesses us with the experience of His presence. Experiencing His presence dramatically changes the perspective on our circumstances. We know we are not alone; we know that Someone bigger and stronger is in control; we have hope for the future—and the "trials turn to joy."

Application: The next time you find yourself in the middle of a difficult time instead of a "blessing," you can rest in the Engineer who is proving to you what He already knows is true of you. He would love for you to see yourself as He sees you—look with the eyes of your heart to see yourself in your mind's eye—sitting on His lap, resting in spite of the difficulties. He is not out to get you; He is not punishing you— He wants you to know who you are and how He sees you. As you "endure" with Him, He will teach you things that are worth more than earthly gold. In the midst of a difficulty, it will feel like it's not ever going to end or get better, but if you persevere, you'll find that something changed for the better—you are stronger, more patient, more mature, more loving and accepting of others; more caring—you know the Engineer.

"Out of the depths, I have cried to Thee, O Lord." "I wait for the Lord, my soul does wait; And in His word do I hope." Psalm 130:1 and 5

There are degrees of trials and difficulties, of course. Broken down cars or a lost phone have little comparison to losing a loved one, getting a divorce, or being told someone has cancer. The pain involved with heavier trials can be very severe and extremely difficult to go through. Oftentimes we might want to run away from, deny or medicate our pain when it feels like it's too much or lasts too long. But we can count on the same intimacy with God and the same faith we have been examining in these devotions to carry us through. He will understand and accept all our feelings without condemning us or being surprised that we hurt so badly. David puts it well (paraphrase mine): "When I found myself in the depths of despair, pain, and hopelessness, the only thing I could do was to wait for the Lord and hope in His word." (Psalm 130:1)

For me, "hope in His word" not only means His words from my Bible, but His words in my heart as verses I have memorized, or a word I know is from Him that pops into my mind. Oftentimes His words come from the mouths of those safe and caring others with whom I share my struggles. Regardless of where the loving, comforting and encouraging words come from, they carry what I know God wants me to know—that I am loved, that He is with me and in me and in control, and that I can trust Him no matter what. While I'm waiting for more light on the subject or the next move to make, I want to have hope. Knowing God is there and that I can talk to Him about anything and everything gives me hope when pain is present.

As you grow in understanding your union with Christ, you will also grow to believe you are hearing God's voice in your mind and heart. His words will bring great comfort in times of suffering. We will look further at how to hear God's voice in the chapter on Feelings and Appearances.

Application: What do you do with painful difficulties—do you turn to God and talk to Him or do you medicate the pain and try to avoid it? God wants to be intimately involved while the difficulties are going on; He wants you to let Him comfort you and show you His great love regardless of your circumstances. It will help you if you take time to be with people who are glad to be with you, who accept you as you are and who will be there without trying to fix your pain. Building up your joy will help you process things and keep going. If things feel too big and too hopeless, you might need to get help from a counselor.

"In that day you shall know that I am in My Father and you in Me, and I in you." John 14:20"

"Seeing" this verse has really helped me feel God's comfort when I'm struggling. I encourage you to follow the directions below to "see it" for yourself. Anabel Gillham taught it something like this:

1) Find four empty envelopes in these sizes and label them with these numbers—large-4, medium-3, small-2, smaller-1.
2) Next label #4 as "God, the Father," Label #3 and #1 as "Jesus," Label #2 as "Me".
3) Now look at the verse above in reverse order:
4) "I in you" - tuck #1 inside #2
5) "You in Me" - tuck #2 inside #3
6) "I am in My Father" - tuck #3 inside #4)

Jesus is in God and we are in Jesus. Then Jesus is in us.[35]

Anything that comes into our lives must come through God, through Jesus, to get to us; and when it gets there, it finds us filled with Jesus—so what is there to fear? What a comforting relief that is when we believe it. Nothing comes to us except what God allows and He is there in us before, during, and after.

> ***Application:*** I encourage you to do this simple exercise with the envelopes and really think about what God is saying here about nothing coming to you without it first going through God and Jesus. Ponder how Jesus surrounds you—you are in Him and He is in you. Memorize Colossians 1:27—". . . Christ in you, the hope of glory."

---

[35] Anabel Gillham, *The Confident Woman*, 1993, Harvest House Publishers, Eugene, OR 97402, page 95

"The light of your body is your eye; therefore when you eye is clear (*single* in the KJV), your whole body also is full of light; but when your eye is bad, your body also is full of darkness." Luke 11:34

Norman Grubb and Dan Stone taught me a new perspective on this verse. It's one that I live by every day, but especially when I'm hurting from trials and struggles. I especially like the King James translation of *single* because it goes along with Genesis 3 where Adam and Eve are facing the forbidden fruit of the tree of the knowledge of good and evil. God had put them in the Garden with all their needs met, but more importantly, they had instant and intimate access to God. Their relationship with God had no barriers and their innocence gave them freedom from worry or guilt. After they ate the forbidden fruit, they became "double" minded, falsely believing that they could be like God and discern good and evil. Instead of innocence, they now carried the burden of sin and guilt and trying to figure out what was right and wrong by themselves.

God provided a way out for Adam and Eve and all of us by sending Jesus to die on the Cross and then come back to life. After we receive Him as Savior, we have the choice to live as our Luke verse tells us. Instead of "double" or "bad" we can and must look at life with a "single eye," an eye that sees only God and His complete authority over everything. As soon as we try to decide what is good and bad apart from God, we feel the darkness of depression, hopelessness and powerlessness.[36] When we keep turning to talk to God again and again in our pain, at first we may not sense His presence and our interactions with Him might be totally by faith with no feelings, but eventually we feel His comforting presence when we calm down enough to remember that He is in control. Living by the "single eye" is one of the most helpful concepts to change how we view painful difficulties that come into our lives, because the single eye turns our focus

---

[36] There are black and white issues in the Scripture such as stealing that we know are right or wrong. In this context we are talking about circumstances that may *feel or look* bad but are not. Or choices might *feel good* that are not. There will be more on this topic in other chapters.

to God instead of the circumstance. Focusing with a "single eye" builds trust as we understand God's love, His sovereignty, and His power.

Application: What is going on in your life right now that you're trying to figure out? Is it frustrating and frightening? Can you look at your circumstance with a single eye that says, "God is in control regardless of how it looks and feels?" Can you keep talking to Him until you sense His comfort and care? Can you trust that He knows all about you and your needs? Ask a trusted friend to pray with you and support you as you learn the "single eye."

"And we know that God causes all things to work together for good to those who love God, to those who are called according to His purpose." Romans 8:28

Paul tells us here in this verse another reason we can trust God and look to Him during trials. He promises to work something for good out of what we might be viewing as bad. When our family first went on staff with Campus Crusade for Christ back in 1976, during the time we were raising support, a friend in Knoxville, Tennessee, was going to loan my husband, Jim, one of his cars. We lived in Huntsville, Alabama, and Jim was going to be spending time in both places. When Jim went by the Barnett's house, to get the car—Bob gave him the car! It was a pristine, one-owner, 1968 Ford Galaxy. Jim was so proud of the car and he and his dad lovingly washed and waxed it.

Two days later, a teenager rear-ended Jim and totaled the car, but it was drivable. Bob and the boy's father had the same insurance company. The next day we received great news! The insurance company told Bob he could have either $950 *or* $850 *and* the car! A circumstance that most would view as bad turned out very well. Jim drove the car home to

Huntsville and Bob sent him the $850 after the insurance company settled. We painted "Romans 8:28" on the smashed up trunk.[37]

> ***Application:*** Can you think of a "Romans 8:28" story in your life? Share it with a friend. This might be a good verse to memorize if you haven't already.

"In this you greatly rejoice even though now for a little while, if necessary, you have been distressed by various trials, that the proof of your faith being more precious than gold, which is perishable, even though tested by fire, may be found to result in praise and glory and honor at the revelation of Jesus Christ; and though you have not seen Him, you love Him, and though you do not see Him now, but believe in Him, you greatly rejoice with joy inexpressible and full of glory, obtaining as the outcome of your faith the salvation of your souls." 1 Peter 1:6-9

Peter has told us in these verses that we can greatly rejoice in a very powerful salvation that even overcomes the sting of difficult circumstances. Through Jesus' love and sacrifice we receive a brand new life full of hope. Our new life here on Earth, and all that comes with it after we die, cannot be destroyed even by trials.

Trials cause us distress when we try to handle them on our own or try to run from the pain. When we avoid the pain that comes with trials and sorrows, it blocks us from getting to know Jesus intimately because we substitute other things such as food, sex, substances and unhealthy relationships to dull the pain. On the other hand, when we turn toward

---

[37] From *Jesus Never Fails*, www.lulu.com/barbaramoon, pages 15-16

Jesus, talk to Him and look to Him for comfort in distressing circumstances, Paul says this will result in faith that is more precious than gold.

Gold is not found in the form of necklaces and rings—it's a rather ugly lump that has to undergo extreme heat in order to be beautiful and useful. What we gain from believing and trusting Jesus during hard times is like refined gold—something that's beautiful, something that lasts, something that's priceless and worth greatly rejoicing over.

We all know that there are degrees of painful circumstances and with some the smelting heat of the pain is more difficult to bear. Losing loved ones, losing our dreams, losing our homes all take longer to get over than "everyday" difficulties. Saying the truth to ourselves does not always take away that kind of heavy pain. At these times when the pain does not go away easily, we have to cry out and talk to Jesus even more, trusting that His promises are true while waiting on His timing and His comfort. In my life, I have trusted Jesus during heavy pain by talking to Him, by journaling and by surrounding myself with close friends or family who bring me joy—they're glad to be with me. When able, I do something fun or spend time with someone who lifts me up in a positive way.

Turning our minds to things we appreciate is a way to get through difficult feelings. Even though we might not be thinking consciously about God, appreciation is connected to Him because the things we appreciate are from God. Thinking about things such as the beauty in nature, the mountains, being at the beach, babies sleeping, or warm blankets make us relax, say "Ahhh" and smile. Appreciation calms us and helps us focus on God[38]. Even when the truth does not take away my pain, I keep saying it to myself and believing it against what I feel. I need support from others to help me keep my eyes on Jesus until I find the "joy inexpressible and full of glory" that Peter says here is true.[39]

---

[38] From *Share Immanuel* booklet, page 6

[39] For more on "Truth does not always take away the pain," see blog by that name at www.barbaramoon.wordpress.com

> *Application:* Right now you may be going through a difficult or even a very painful circumstance that is hard to bear. Even though you cannot see Jesus, cry out to Him and talk to Him about what you are feeling. He is always glad to be with you and He wants you to know His presence even if the pain does not go away for a while. Like gold being refined, if you keep turning to Jesus, I can assure you that your pain will bring you the intimacy that makes for "inexpressible joy."

"Blessed be the God and Father of our Lord Jesus Christ, the Father of mercies and God of all comfort; who comforts us in all our affliction so that we may be able to comfort those who are in any affliction with the comfort with which we ourselves are comforted by God. For just as the sufferings of Christ are ours in abundance, so also our comfort is abundant through Christ." 2 Corinthians 1: 3-5

"Look! The virgin will conceive a child! She will give birth to a son, and they will call him Immanuel, which means 'God is with us.'" Matthew 1:23 *New Living Translate*

When we are in the middle of a painful situation or trial, what Paul calls here an "affliction," sometimes not much of anything seems to help us feel better. Jesus, Immanuel (God with us),[40] is always there but we may not perceive His presence, we may not turn to Him, or we may not even want to hear truth. This is the point where we can either remember that He wants to comfort us or we might be sorely tempted to turn to something else to dull the pain. Turning to something else is how we can

---

[40] Matthew 28:20; Hebrews 13:5

get trapped by using substances or overeating or withdrawing from others. He wants to comfort us; He wants us to sense His presence.

One of the ways we can learn to sense Jesus' presence is by remembering a time when we *did* sense He was there. It might even be at the time that we invited Him into our life. When we go back to a time that we *did* sense His presence and sit quietly for a few minutes, we can then ask Jesus to show us where He is with us in the *present* moment. This makes it easier to pray and talk to Him and hear what He wants us to know.[41] If we trust that He is there and that He is speaking, we will find both comfort and His perspective on our affliction. His very comforting presence in times of suffering is our main path to intimacy. We will have abundant sufferings in this life, but we can experience His abundant comfort any time.

Application: What do you do with your emotional pain? Do you medicate it or try to find comfort by talking to Jesus or a close friend? Allow Jesus to meet you there and go through it with you. He knows and understands better than anyone else. He wants to heal the roots of your pain and set you free from them.

"Rejoice with those who rejoice, and weep with those who weep." Romans 12: 15

Here is a great way to look at what this verse says: "No one has to fix anyone's pain; we just need to sit with them in it. It cannot be fixed; it can only be healed."[42] Sitting with someone does not mean that we are silent—

---

[41] For more information on Immanuel's presence and healing, see *Share Immanuel* booklet by Dr. Wilder and Chris Coursey, available at www.lifemodel.org and www.thrivetoday.org

it means we don't try to fix them with clichés, Bible verses, truth or corrections. We validate their hurt and comfort with voice tone and comforting words. After the pain is relieved a little, then hurting people can better hear truth or guidance about what is causing their pain.

When we hurt with someone, and communicate that we're glad to be with them during their pain instead of trying to fix their pain, it communicates to them that they have great value. When we share their pain, and they don't have to suffer alone, it teaches them they don't have to fear pain. Un-comforted pain, un-validated pain that is not considered important by another is the single largest reason people do not mature. Without validation and comfort, people get stuck and stop growing in that area where the pain occurred. Any time someone does not receive what they need, they hurt. Without comfort, they learn to fear pain and then avoid it through addictions.[43]

When you hurt with someone else in their pain, even though you don't enjoy it, eventually it will help you realize the places you lacked comfort for your own pain. It might bring up some pain that you need validated. You will realize that it really did hurt and you needed someone to hurt with you. As you realize and face your hurts, you will find healing as well.

Sitting with others in their pain without trying to fix them is very comforting and healing. When we experience comfort, either from God or "Jesus with skin on," (a human person who is with us and helping us) we learn that we are valuable and that pain does not have to be feared, which makes it easier to ask for comfort the next time.

Application: How do you handle others' pain—are you able to just sit with them without fixing them? Are you learning for yourself that your pain shows how valuable you are?

---

[42] From Dr. Wilder in a phone conversation. See my book, *Joy-Filled Relationships* at amazon.com for more on this topic.

[43] From Dr. Wilder in a phone conversation.

"...who comforts us in all our affliction so that we will be able to comfort those who are in any affliction with the comfort with which we ourselves are comforted by God." 2 Corinthians 1: 4

Paul is telling us here that later, after we have experienced the comfort of Jesus, we will be able to help others who are hurting. The hurts that we've felt and had comforted do not have to be the same as what another person is feeling; the comfort we received from Jesus can be passed on to another with "any affliction." It's simply the fact that we have experienced His comfort that enables us to understand and empathize with others' hurts.

In 1994, when I first began talking to Dr. Wilder about my painful circumstances, I discovered that I knew very little about what to do with painful wounds and memories. I did not have substance addictions, but I was good at avoiding pain by staying busy or trying to get others to like me. During that time I gained a totally different view of suffering and trials.

One of the most life-changing truths I learned is that "pain means comfort is on the way."[44] I had never heard anyone say this and seldom find anyone now who knows it. Most of us have learned to avoid pain if we got little comfort growing up. In reality, because few understand it, when I share this quote, I want to say, "Pain is *supposed to* mean comfort is on the way." But I have come to realize that when relationships work as God intends, we will not need to fear pain because we will learn that comfort follows pain.

Understanding that "pain means comfort is on the way" takes the sting out of our afflictions and prepares us to comfort others with the comfort we have received from God.

---

[44] From conversations with Dr. Wilder

© 2013 Barbara Moon

"That I might know Him and the power of His resurrection and the fellowship of His sufferings, being conformed to His death." Philippians 3:10

Years ago while on Campus Crusade staff, our team took time for a day with the Lord, and the passage I chose to go through was this passage in Philippians. I truly wanted to know His power in my life. Suddenly, the phrase "fellowship of His sufferings" jumped out at me. "Oh, Dear," I thought. "Paul seems to be saying that the way to His power is through suffering and death."

Off and on through the years, I have come to understand these words in various ways. I learned about my death on the Cross with Christ; (See devotion on Galatians 2:20 in Grace and Union.) I came to the end of living the Christian life in my own efforts, a sort of death, and I have experienced the fellowship of His sufferings as I turned to Him during, disappointment, painful rejection, and hardships. Because I had a bent towards allowing people to put me down without defending myself, in some relationships I had confusion about the difference between loving others unconditionally and allowing someone to harm me.

I learned the difference in biblical suffering—"the fellowship of His sufferings"—and allowing others to harm me with their actions or words. Here are some of the ways I learned to distinguish the two:[45]

---

[45] These truths are from conversations with Dr. Wilder

- Suffering is something godly that we desire to do, something that fits with God's kind of love described in I Corinthians 13. For example if your child was running out into the street and helping him required you to suffer in some way, wild horses could not keep you from doing it.

- When we are being beaten up, whether verbally or physically, we want to get away. We feel that inner struggle to get away from harm because it's an evil thing to harm someone. There's a difference in hurt and harm—the dentist hurts me to help me, but he does not harm. Test the feeling internally—if wild horses cannot keep you from doing it, then it's godly and biblical suffering. Allowing yourself to be harmed is not biblical suffering and you need to get away.

- Godly suffering endures hardship so others might know who they are.[46] Hardships are inconveniences, difficulties, annoyances, living humbly. We endure things such as these for the sake of another person. Think about Jesus, the disciples and Paul—all that they went through for us to know who we are—children of God.

- When you want to get away from someone who is hurting you—go. If you're diving under water, holding your breath, eventually you want to get a breath. This does not mean you won't ever dive again. It's all right to leave a harmful situation in order to get a message across that you refuse to be mistreated. You can go back when the situation is better.

- If you are in a bathtub of scalding hot water, you do not stay in the tub and say, "I'm committed to cleanliness." You get out of the tub until the water cools down.[47]

Knowing these truths helps us understand the times we need to stand up for ourselves and potentially remove ourselves from a situation, versus

---

[46] *The Red Dragon Cast Down,* E. James Wilder, p. 286

[47] In a letter from Dr. Wilder

the times when we are called to love unconditionally. It's not an easy route to walk and takes time to learn when to say things that need to be said and do what needs to be done so that we know our suffering is godly.

> ***Application:*** I encourage you to think about what wild horses will not keep you from doing when something painful comes up. Making the choice to suffer in those instances will be godly suffering. But if you are being mistreated—go away and look at your situation in light of taking care of yourself and not allowing someone to harm a valuable you. Get support to do what you need to do to get away from harm. Also, there can be another aspect of suffering that is a blend of these two: There are things that happen to us that are not our choice and that we cannot get away from—until later. Whatever your situation might be, seek help if you're unsure.

"Now I rejoice in my sufferings for your sake, and in my flesh I do my share on behalf of His body (which is the church) in filling up that which is lacking in Christ's afflictions." Colossians 1:24

Keeping in mind the difference between godly suffering and allowing harm, let's consider what the Apostle Paul means when he says that we can "rejoice in our sufferings." The joy we encounter in godly suffering does not mean that we are happy to suffer; the joy comes from what happens when we talk to Jesus and learn His perspectives during the difficult circumstances. The better you know Jesus and connect with Him, the better you will move towards seeing the possibility of being able to "rejoice in my sufferings" like Paul talks about in the verse above. It's all right to be growing in this area. It's all right to feel what we need to feel. It's all right to struggle with rejoicing during a trial.

Rejoicing in suffering does not mean that we stay in an abusive relationship where we are being harmed. When abuse is going on, we need outside help to determine what steps to take. This devotion is about opportunities we have to suffer well in hard situations and how that can help us grow in intimacy with Jesus and continue to develop godly character. Abuse is a different matter.

Here is another way I grew to better understand biblical suffering from Dr. Wilder: When we suffer, we're bringing the same message to the world as Jesus did. Jesus suffered because we are so valuable; we are worth dying for. It's common for good parents to wish they could take their child's place when the child is sick. That's what He did. We defend and want to help those we love because of their value. As Paul is telling us here, when we suffer for the sake of others, we are like Jesus to our world—showing people we cherish them and how valuable they are. ("This is my commandment that you love one another, just as I have loved you." John 15: 12; "Truly I say to you, to the extent that you did it to one of these brothers of Mine, even the least of them, you did it to Me." Matthew 25:40)

Sometimes it helps to know that part of our suffering is identification with Christ's suffering, that it's for us to grow and for us to help others.

Application: Have you experienced a very difficult time in your life that brought you into more intimacy with Jesus? Have you seen God use a time of suffering in your life to help someone else in theirs? Think about the idea that your suffering is for the sake of Christ and His people. Allow your suffering to show you your value and be open to opportunities to help others in their pain.

"We are pressed on every side by troubles, but we are not crushed. We are perplexed, but not driven to despair. We are hunted down, but never abandoned by God. We get knocked down, but we are not destroyed. Through suffering, our bodies continue to share in the death of Jesus so that the life of Jesus may also be seen in our bodies." II Corinthians 4:8-10 *New Living Translation*

Paul tells us here in this passage that not only are we a "stand-in" for Christ in our suffering, but also God is right there with us in our trials and He is using them to make us more like Christ. As Christians, on the *inside*, we are holy, perfect and blameless. When we allow them to, trials mold us on the *outside* so that others can see Christ in us. When we've found God's comfort in our suffering, we will show more empathy for others who are hurting. We will be softer and more tender towards others. If we have suffered consequences for bad choices, we will not put others down who are struggling, but rather we will desire to help them get through their difficulties.

Most of us conclude when we're suffering that it means we don't have value. Our view of God is that we don't matter or else He would not make us suffer. When we think that way, we tend to not appreciate others' value either. If we stop and think about it, we only hurt and grieve over valuable things. There is no sorrow over garbage or discards. When evil (injury) collides with value it equals pain. The greater the capacity to feel the pain reveals the greater value. If evil collides with evil it has no problem and there is no pain.[48] As we come to understand our value because of our suffering, we will kick less against the situations that come into our lives. We will have a different perspective on our own pain which will result in intimacy with Jesus and more love towards others. Others will notice our peace, our empathy and our love towards them—they will see Jesus.

Application: Are you beginning to see how valuable you are to God that He would send godly suffering your way? It takes some

---

[48] From conversations with Dr. Wilder

consideration, but realizing the positives about suffering can be very life-changing. Think about a place where you've suffered and ask Jesus to show you His perspective on it. If you think that you're in an abusive situation, please get help. It will also help to bear suffering if you do things to keep your joy level up by being with people who love you and are glad to be with you no matter what you're feeling. Take time out to "play" with others after you hurt and get some comfort. (Video games and other "escapes" don't really count as play.)

"Yes, we live under constant danger of death because we serve Jesus, so that the life of Jesus will be evident in our dying bodies. So we live in the face of death, but this has resulted in eternal life for you." II Corinthians 4:11-12 *New Living Translation*.

Paul continues to speak about the positives of suffering, telling us here that "the life of Jesus will be evident" to others when His character is built into our lives. When something hurts us, we can use that hurt to find one of the characteristics of our new heart that Jesus gave us. For example if we're hurting because someone betrays us, then we value being loyal. If we hurt when someone tells us a lie, then this shows we are honest. When we hurt, looking for the opposite characteristics is another way to help turn the hurt into a positive. It's like you to hurt when someone hurts you in a way that is opposite to a characteristic of your heart.[49]

Satan does not like for us to know these positive characteristics of our heart nor does he want us to live them out. He knows if we "get in trouble" while living from our heart, we are less likely to live out that characteristic. For example, if you get negative reactions from others when you say what needs to be said, you will lean towards not being honest with your words.

---

[49] Barbara Moon, *Joy Filled Relationships,* 2012, www.amazon.com, page 217

If you "get in trouble" for being a diligent worker, you may start to slack off. If you get rejected for refusing to "go along with the crowd," you may compromise your integrity. It's easier to defend against the enemy's attacks when you know who you are and what your heart is like. [50]

I saw the importance of naming heart characteristics one night at a small group meeting when one of the ladies was very upset with herself because a family member rejected her constantly. My friend had done all she knew to do to keep the relationship with her sister, but to no avail. As she talked about her painful feelings and how upset she was with herself that she could not fix the situation, I said to her, "If you are so upset because of this rejection, that tells us that you are a very accepting person. 'Accepting' is one of the characteristics of your heart." Immediately my friend began to weep softly. Deep in her heart she saw that her very pain of feeling rejected was proof of one of her wonderful characteristics. Her perspective on the rejection and her inability to fix the situation changed.

> *Application:* Think of a place or time when you seem to "get into trouble" with other people. Perhaps you get fussed at or rejected. What is the heart characteristic that the enemy does not want you to live out? What are the things that hurt you? What are the opposites of those things? These are all characteristics of your heart.

---

[50] *Jewels for My Journey*, page 139; Ideas from Dr. Wilder

"When therefore Jesus saw His mother, and the disciple whom He loved standing nearby, He said to His mother, 'Woman, behold your son!' Then He said to the disciple, 'Behold your mother!' And from that hour the disciple took her into his own household." John 19: 26-27

While we are talking about heart characteristics and the differences between biblical suffering and harm, let's look at some barriers we can encounter that prevent us from "suffering well." Suffering well means that when we're hurting, we are able to stay relational with other people and act like ourselves—we're able to live out our heart characteristics in spite of difficult emotions. Jesus on the Cross is our best example of suffering well. He stayed relational as always in spite of the suffering. In these verses here we see how He loved His mother and made certain she would be cared for. We know also that He talked with the thief crucified by His side and He sang Psalms. Jesus "suffered well" in spite of His extreme emotions and pain.[51]

I see a tendency in our day to go the opposite route when difficulties occur. We often mistake godly suffering and love for an unhealthy kind of love that is now called "co-dependency." Co-dependency is a distorted form of love that causes someone to keep another person from feeling his or her pain for various reasons. Sometimes we keep them from feeling their pain because we will be uncomfortable, we don't want to see them hurt, or they will get angry if we say something they don't want to hear. (The co-dependent person will not address bad behavior in the other.) Sometimes we help them avoid pain by not allowing them to pay consequences for their actions. (A co-dependent wife calls the office to say her drunk husband is sick. A mother lets her grown son sleep all day instead of working.) These are examples of enabling someone to avoid feeling what they need to feel because they don't have to pay consequences.

Unlike Jesus who took all upon Himself yet cared for others in a healthy way, co-dependents often feel others' feelings for them by allowing themselves to be harmed when others are upset. When the co-

---

[51] From conversations with Dr. Wilder and in *Joy Filled Relationships*, page 78.

dependent allows the harm out of fear, the offender does not have to take responsibility for his or her actions and the offended one remains in an abusive relationship. It appears that the offended one is loving the abuser during his or her difficulties, but in truth that kind of "suffering" is not biblical suffering. It's quite common for the co-dependent to act out this unhealthy kind of "love" because he or she is so desperate to feel important, wanted and special. We will look more at co-dependency in the chapter on Rest and Peace.

Application: Are you able, most of the time, to stay relational and act like your usual self when circumstances are difficult? Do you ever find yourself trying to keep another person from feeling their feelings and paying their own consequences? Ask God to show you any unhealthy ways you are trying to love others.

"Weeping may last for the night, but a shout of joy comes in the morning." Psalm 30: 5b

Sometimes when we're hurting it feels like nothing is going to get better; it's going to hurt forever. We still turn to Jesus even when we feel like He is not listening.

When the Lights Stay Off[52]

Some people call it the "dark night of the soul" when we're weeping in the night and cannot seem to see an end. Nothing feels like it used to when the lights were on. Some days the sun is shining, but the Son is mostly quiet. Questions buzz. Thoughts

---

[52] www.barbaramoon.wordpress.com

whir. Nothing seems to work. Once in a while, the shadows fade when a little light breaks through.

I turn to Jesus, writing in my journal, seeking His face in the middle of this current "dark night:"[53]

"I've been here before when I went through the divorce," I tell myself, "—and on the other side it's magnificent and worth the cost, because I know You so much deeper."

"I know what I know," I assure myself, "—God is here and He knows what He's doing. I know You are here, Lord, because You promised to never leave me. I can't feel You right now, but I know You're here because You keep Your word."

"Let someone know how bad it is," I order myself. "—ask for help. This is too hard to feel by yourself. There are many who care and some who can bear to be here with you. They will help you hold on to truth."

I hear Jesus whisper: *All things work together for good. [54]* I listen.

There may be pain in the night, but joy comes in the morning.[55]

Joy. Is it only a feeling? I ask. *No. Joy is a Person. I am your joy.[56]* When is the morning? I reply.

Not until I say it's morning. Can I make the dawn break? *No. There's no use in trying.*

I love you. I am Immanuel and I am here. I am working in the dark. Darkness and light are alike to Me.[57] He speaks a verse I've hidden in my heart.

---

[53] My old friend, Dan Stone said it feels like God is off somewhere drinking lemonade when we struggle to find God's light again.

[54] Romans 8:28

[55] Psalm 30:5

[56] Galatians 5:22

[57] Psalm 139:12c

I am Joy and I am always glad to be with you. Cling to Me. Don't fret. Feel the feelings. I am feeling all of it with you. We are one.[58]

I want the lights to be on, illuminating the questions, stilling the whirring. That would feel so much better. But for now I believe by faith that the Son is shining—even in the dark.

God can make good use of all that happens. But the loss is real." C. S. Lewis[59]

Application: What do you do when you feel like the lights have gone out and God is not there? Do you get angry with Him? Do you turn to Him anyway and see what He wants you to know?

"Therefore, since Christ has suffered in the flesh, arm yourselves also with the same purpose, because he who has suffered in the flesh has ceased from sin." 1 Peter 4:1

During the difficult time in my life when I was talking to Dr. Wilder weekly, he helped me understand the pain I was feeling. Losses were huge and many aspects of my life had changed. Because of all the pain, there were days when I felt there was something wrong with me. I wondered why the pain just kept on and on. I asked Dr. Wilder what was wrong with me. He gave a very interesting answer using this verse from 1 Peter:

---

[58] I Corinthians 6:17

[59] *Perelandra*

There is nothing wrong with you. That is an insult to God. What is *right* with you is what hurts. We are at a point where all you are going through should hurt like this.

There is room to go wrong now if you reject your capacity to hurt like this. Grow through the pain to embracing your capacity to hurt. When your suffering is done you will be 'without sin.' (1 Peter 4:1) When you freely embrace the hurt, you will have nothing to fear or be scared of.

Tearing loved ones from His heart would feel the same way to God. To turn away would be wrong. If you reach the highest level saturated with pain, embrace and hold on to it, not just to the pain, but to yourself—to yourself who can hurt that way.

God is perfecting you—a person of deep value. If you didn't hurt or weren't bothered, you wouldn't be the person you are. Bring every bit of the hurt in, don't miss a part.[60]

It's difficult to put into words how learning to feel my emotional pain changed my life. No one had ever shown me how or told me why it was beneficial. When I faced my fear of hurting and allowed myself to feel what I needed to feel, I understood that being able to hurt showed my value. It meant that I was a loving, caring person who could not just slough off pain. The result was that I no longer feared hurting. Now when suffering comes, I talk to Jesus, I cry, I let the hurt come without fear. I know it will take me deeper with Jesus. It's not pleasant to hurt like that, but intimacy with Jesus makes it worth every tear.

After I learned to go through my hurts without avoiding them, I had a new appreciation for others' painful moments. Sometimes I have to remind myself not to try to put band aids of truth said too quickly on others' hurts, but generally I respond with empathy and the desire to sit with them. Later I can help them find Jesus in their pain. Avoiding pain does not heal anything or help us grow. Going through the pain and finding Jesus'

---

[60] *Jewels for My Journey*, page 132

perspective, love, and comfort brings the peace and intimacy for which we long—and heals the pain.

> ***Application:*** Even though this concept is difficult to grasp, consider that your suffering shows your value; it shows that you are loving and sensitive, not hardened and without feelings. As you feel your feelings instead of avoiding them, you will be more like Jesus and fear of pain will be gone.

"For it was fitting for Him, for whom are all things, and through whom are all things in bringing many sons to glory to perfect the author of their salvation through sufferings." Hebrews 2:10

"Although He was a Son, He learned obedience from the things which He suffered." Hebrews 5:8

As we continue to look at how to find joy in intimacy with God through how we handle pain, let's look again at how pain shows us our value. We have Jesus as our example. Once after talking with Dr. Wilder on the phone when things were particularly painful, he prayed: "Lord God, Speak the truth to Barbara about the pain. Show her how every time You send her another opportunity to hurt that You are doing a great thing to show Barbara her value."

The prayer stirred my thinking to wonder aloud to Dr. Wilder, "Are you saying pain shows our value because of what Jesus did on the Cross? Is it like that?"

> "Yes, it is," Dr. Wilder answered softy. "Only something good and holy would hurt like this. Your capacity to love has to be equal to your hurt. You love greatly or you wouldn't hurt like this. It's proof of who you are and how full of love you are. It's in

© 2013 Barbara Moon

every part of you— your body, your soul, your emotions. It's a purifying process in you and all that will be left is love. It will sound like nonsense if you try to share it with others. If God hadn't sustained you, you would not be here. (Psalm 119: 116) [61]

Application: I pray that as you think on these verses about suffering that you will come to see it is a privilege to take His yoke and learn of Him (Matthew 11:29, devotion in Rest and Peace)—to take up what is lacking in the afflictions of Christ (Colossians 1:24, devotion above) — to know how full of love you are because you know how much you hurt. The Master is shaping His vessel for intimacy and service.

"Though He slay me, yet will I trust Him. . ." Job 13:15 KJV

Recently I received an email from my niece, Michelle. Michelle was troubled by a question that plagues most of us when something tragically painful happens: "Why did God let this happen?" I was honored to try to give words to Michelle in her grief, knowing that words do not always help. While answering her letter, God reminded me of Job, the Old Testament character with whom most of us associate trials and suffering. Here is an excerpt from my response to Michelle, broken up into two parts:

Part One

Dear Michelle, I am honored that you have written in this terrible time of pain you are feeling alongside this grieving mother. There are not a lot of words that will give you comfort, but I will try. There truly

---

[61] *Jewels for My Journey*, page 132

is nothing more painful than the death of a child, no matter the age. It shows how valuable *you* are that you are able to hurt like this. It's like you, Michelle, to hurt like this. Only valuable things hurt. We don't worry and hurt much about un-valuable things.

Of course, like many others, you question why and how. I have found that God does not answer many "why" questions, but He does answer questions more like, "What do you want me to know about this?' And He answers, "Where were You when this happened?"[62] We often think He was not there in a painful event because of the outcome, but He is always with us and never leaves us. When we "see" that He was there for a terrible event, we will see that He is hurting right along with us, He is feeling what we feel. That helps a little, but the why is hard to deal with.

Sometimes we say that bad things happen to good people because the world has been damaged by sin and these are part of the Fall in the Garden. That is part of the reason, but not very comforting. One thing I do not say is that a person is being punished.

"I have heard of Thee by the hearing of the ear; but now my eye sees Thee." Job 42:5

Part Two

When we look at Job in the Bible we see that Job had three friends who came to try to help him when all his children and all his land were taken away. First we see that when Satan came to talk to God it was God who brought up Job. God did give Satan permission, and since we're human we cannot always know why. Job remained true to God, but his friends told him: 1) It's your own fault—religion is the way out (chap. 4-5); It's sin in your life—tradition is the way out (chap.8); If you would straighten up all would be ok—common sense is the way out (Chap.11) Some of the friends came at Job again with other accusations such as to repent or to reject God.

---

[62] Questions learned from Dr. Wilder. For more information see the *Share Immanuel* booklet, Shepherd's House www.lifemodel.org or www.thrivetoday.org

In Job 13:15 we find one of Job's responses to his not-so-helpful friends. To me it says the most about trusting God in our painful moments—it's the verse we used above—"Though He slay me, Yet will I trust Him." The real questions for our aching hearts are, "What am I going to do with God when these terrible things happen? Am I going to trust Him or turn away from Him?"

After the bad counselors finish with Job, the youngest friend, Elihu comes to speak to Job. He affirms God's goodness several times. (Ch. 33-36) Finally after being rather quiet the whole time, God comes and speaks to Job. What God is doing and showing Job culminates in Chapter 42 verse 5 when Job says, "I have heard of Thee by the hearing of the ear; but now my eye sees Thee. . ." Job mainly knew God by hearsay, in his head, not by experience. Now Job sees God with new eyes, the eyes of the spirit, in his heart; by experience.

In my life and experience, this is what I have learned to see about pain—if we cling to Jesus and allow Him to do whatever He needs to do, our pain will bring intimacy with Him beyond our dreams. It's often pain from losses that truly bring us to Him and we find how real He is. He is as real as anything you can touch or see. We have two choices—to get mad at God and run away from Him, or trust His sovereignty and that He *is* love and cannot do anything but love.

So I think maybe that's why when we see where He was in a painful event, we see Him sharing, validating and comforting our pain instead of telling us why it happened.

This is the gist of my answer, though I do know words don't help the pain. You can only go through it and hold on to Jesus. You will know Him better during and after. Remember, "Pain means comfort is on the way," "Pain means you are valuable or you wouldn't hurt," (think of Jesus on the Cross) and "Pain means Jesus is on the way."

I love you and am honored to respond. Anytime. Love, Aunt Barbara

Application: Like so many, maybe you have asked this same question and wondered why bad things happen. Think on the truths presented here and ask Jesus to show you how to look at these kinds of situations. Let Him teach you that "pain means comfort is on the way." He wants to validate and comfort your pain with His presence.

"And the LORD said, 'Shall I hide from Abraham what I am about to do?'" Genesis 18:17

As we look at learning to feel and go through our hurts, this verse from Genesis gives us a little balance. God debated about hiding from Abraham what He was about to do to Sodom and Gomorrah. [63] Sometimes we, too, have to find the right time and place to process our pain. It's helpful to understand the difference in avoiding pain and in waiting to process it appropriately.

When we're in a lot of pain, God wants us to acknowledge the hurt and feel it, not stuff or repress it. Avoiding pain leads to addictions, one important reason for learning to feel and go through our emotional pain. If we do not get comfort during pain growing up, we inadvertently learn to turn to something that will make the pain feel better, something that substitutes pleasure for relational joy and comfort. Over the years, without loving comfort from a person when we hurt, whatever pleasurable things we turn to that calm our hurts—food, sex, excitement, seeking love in wrong ways and places—these pleasure-substitutes become addictions.

On the other hand, feeling our emotional pain does not mean that we show it to everyone all the time. You may have to hide some of the hurt from certain people, like children, or others that can't bear it. That's different than rejecting or denying the pain. We need safe, mature people to help us through our painful memories and moments. If we are going

---

[63] *Jewels for My Journey*, pages 131-132

through a trial and we have to function and work or take care of family, it's not "stuffing" to put something "on the back burner" to look at when it's too big for the moment or likely to affect others who are not able to help us process. Everyone cannot handle extreme emotions. Save processing time for people with maturity and the capacity to help you.

Application: Do you have a mature and trustworthy person to help you with strong emotions? Do you suffer with addictions that are hurting you and making relationships difficult? God wants to heal you and set you free. Talk to Him about whatever it is that you need.

"Consider it all joy my brethren, when you encounter various trials, knowing that the testing (proving) of your faith produces endurance, and let endurance have its perfect result that you may be perfect and complete, lacking in nothing." James 1:1 and 2

Now that we've spent some time considering how to look at suffering, it's my prayer that you will be better able to "consider it all joy, when you encounter various trials." The next time you face a painful trial, turn to Jesus—He is always there and waiting to validate your feelings and comfort you. The more you learn to turn to Him and hold on to Him and believe He loves you in spite of circumstances, the deeper you will go in the intimacy with Christ that you desire. Trials and suffering, though difficult to endure, can be one of the best ways to experience His love and comfort. His love and comfort lead to intimacy.

INTIMACY THROUGH FORGIVENESS

"Let all bitterness and wrath and anger and clamor and slander be put away from you along with all malice. And be kind one to another, tender hearted, forgiving one another, just as God in Christ has also forgiven you." Ephesians 4:31-32

We've considered how to increase intimacy with Christ through faith, salvation, union, freedom from the law and suffering. Now let's take a look at another ingredient—forgiveness. Forgiveness is a subject about which much has been written, and one of the most vital ingredients of a good relationship, whether with God or other people. When forgiveness is neglected as a daily exercise, walls of un-forgiveness, mortared with bitterness, anger, and hate can negatively affect our relationships with one another and God. When there is un-forgiveness in our hearts, the result is that we expend a lot of energy that could go to better uses.

I see three important aspects of forgiveness: *Granting Forgiveness, Receiving Forgiveness* and *Seeking Forgiveness.* Considering these three will help us look at how freedom and intimacy are possible when forgiveness is a way of life. We will see the bondage and ill health that result from un-forgiveness and how to tear down the walls that are built and maintained through pride, doubt, and guilt. We will also see that a necessary ingredient to all three of these facets of forgiveness is the virtue of humility. Growing in humility will be a natural result of practicing forgiveness as we follow God's patterns and instructions spoken of in the Scriptures. It is impossible to seek forgiveness without humbling oneself and admitting wrong. Humility is just as necessary when granting or receiving forgiveness.

Application: Do you struggle with seeking forgiveness from those you have offended? Do you struggle with forgiving those who have offended you? Talk to Jesus about your struggle and allow Him to show you the importance of humbling yourself and seeking or granting forgiveness when necessary.

". . . But You are a God of forgiveness, gracious and compassionate, slow to anger and abounding in loving-kindness; and you did not forsake them." Nehemiah 9:17

"If You, LORD, should mark iniquities, O Lord, who could stand; But there is forgiveness with You that You may be feared." Psalm 130:3-4

These verses tell us what we have already looked at through Christ's work on the Cross—God is a God of forgiveness. Included in Christ's work is the fact that, because He has forgiven us and He lives in us, we have the power and motivation to continue His work of forgiveness with one another. God does not keep track of our iniquities, but forgives them. We stand in reverential awe (fear) of our God who has such love, and we want to pass it to others.

I love these verses that emphasize God's love and forgiveness from the Old Testament. It seems that many people believe God is angry and full of wrath. That is a side of Him when sin is concerned, but He is also full of compassion and loving-kindness. In the New Testament we see that He poured out His wrath on Jesus. We are forgiven and can pass that on to others.

"For if you forgive men for their transgressions, your heavenly Father will also forgive you. But if you do not forgive men, then your Father will not forgive your transgressions." Matthew 6:14, 15

"And when you were dead in your transgressions and the un-circumcision of your flesh, He made you alive together with Him, having forgiven us all our transgressions." Colossians 2: 13

Through the years, Matthew 6:14-15 has been a confusing verse to me. I know that Christ's work on the Cross is total and sufficient; that we are forgiven for past, present, and future sins. In Matthew, Jesus had not yet died. The Colossians verse emphasizes what Christ has done and how it affects us who believe in Him. All our transgressions are forgiven. So what does the Matthew verse mean?

It seems that this verse is more about fellowship with God and other people than it is about salvation. Un-confessed and un-forgiven sin causes walls and lack of connection. The Father wants us to make things right with each other. Jesus came to save, redeem and restore.

Think about a family where two brothers are having conflict, they're too angry to work it out, so each is sent to his room. Dad and Mom are not happy with the conflict and everyone is affected and out of sorts. Dad's love doesn't change, but neither is he going to take sides and be okay with one son and not the other. He wants the whole family to be reconnected, to be glad to be together, and to be on the same track again. The forgiveness is there wrapped in the Dad's love, but until the brothers forgive and return to joy with each other, the Dad's fellowship is not the same with either one. He can't display the forgiveness wrapped in his love until they forgive each other.

God has forgiven us and given us a new life through Christ—we were dead and now He has made us alive. The Psalmist tells us that our sins are as far away as the East is from the West. (Psalm 103:12) Jesus tells us to treat others as He treats us. (Matthew 7:12) Our Heavenly Father wants His family to forgive, reconnect, and stay in fellowship. Forgiveness is a main ingredient.

So as we explore the aspects of forgiveness, I believe it will help if we first look at some things that forgiveness is not, some things it is, and some questions about forgiveness. We will see the reasons for continuing His work of forgiveness with one another. (Romans 5: 6-8) The result will be intimacy with Christ and others.

Application: Keep an open mind about forgiveness as we look at its different aspects. There may be some ideas that are new to you. Your Heavenly Father wants intimate fellowship with you and forgiveness is an important ingredient.

"**And be kind one to another, tender hearted, forgiving one another, just as God in Christ has also forgiven you.**" **Ephesians 4:32**

Forgiveness is not:

Although forgiveness is a key part of maintaining intimacy with God and others, forgiveness is not saying that what someone did to hurt us okay. It is not condoning their actions. Many people deny themselves better relationships and peace of mind because they incorrectly believe these two concepts. Overlooking hurts only causes them to fester. Forgiveness is not overlooking or condoning another's actions; forgiveness bursts the boil of bitterness and lets it heal.

If we try to suppress a hurt and avoid forgiving by saying it doesn't matter, that is a lie. Hurts and wounds are painful and should be acknowledged as such, and when the relationship warrants, discussed. Discussing hurts takes maturity and humility from both people. When possible, it's helpful to say something like, "What you did hurt me and it's hard to be close to you because of the hurt. I want to be close. Can we try to work this out?" When we say that something hurts, we're telling the truth—we're not saying it's okay. Even if we have to forgive without discussing the hurt, we need to admit it hurt, and then choose to forgive. We will look further at this.

Forgiveness is:

Getting these misconceptions of forgiveness out of the way helps us be able to forgive, and forgiving becomes even more significant when we understand what forgiveness really is. Whether we are forgiving another person for something they did that hurt us or something they failed to do that hurt us, forgiveness is about choosing to let go of the hurt or wound or failure and no longer holding it against the other person. Forgiveness is an act of the will that we do for *ourselves* in order to be free from grudges and bitterness. Bitterness destroys.

"See to it that no one comes short of the grace of God that no root of bitterness springing up causes trouble, and by it many be defiled. : Hebrews 12:15

Why forgive?

Holding onto grudges consumes tremendous amounts of energy which can result in depression. It also gives ground for the enemy to mess with our lives and can negatively affect our worship of God. (Matthew 5:23-24.) Un-forgiveness breeds bitterness which affects our fellowship with one another. We choose to forgive, not only because God says to, but because lack of forgiveness harms our relationships, our mental health, and like jealousy and envy, even our physical health. (Proverbs 14:30)

Maybe you have seen the movie or play *Les Misèrables.* The policeman, Javert, is a prime example of what un-forgiveness does to a person. Because Javert believes that all laws must be kept or punished regardless of grace and mercy, he lives a miserable life without love and relationships. In the end, when shown grace by Valjean, Javert takes his own life rather than receive or grant forgiveness. On the other hand, Valjean is a prime example of how forgiveness works when granted and received. After being forgiven, Valjean lives a life full of love.[64]

Application: Do you see the importance of forgiving so that you won't become bitter. Consider whom you might need to forgive in order for your own mind, heart, and body to be healthy. We will look at a way to forgive later in the chapter.

"Then Peter came and said to Him, 'Lord, how often shall my brother sin against me and I forgive him? Up to seven times?' Jesus said to him, 'I do not say to you, up to seven times, but up to seventy times seven.'" Matthew 18: 21-22

When do we forgive?

When someone has hurt us, the best way to return to joy and fellowship is if they ask our forgiveness. But this is not a necessary ingredient in order for us to forgive, and it depends on the other person doing something they may or may not do. We do not have to wait to be asked. We grant forgiveness as an act of our will and forgive the same way

---

[64] See www.barbaramoon.wordpress.com for blogs *Musings on Les Misèrables*

God does—unconditionally. As I consider when to forgive, I picture two scenarios. The first is the practice of forgiving on a "daily" basis within normal relating situations. As we go through the day, it's easy to ignore someone or snap at someone impatiently or answer a question with sarcasm that hurts. Those daily kinds of exchanges should be dealt with immediately. If I'm the one who growls, I quickly seek forgiveness. (For how, see that section.) If someone else hurts me, even if they don't seek forgiveness, I forgive them. It would be good to talk about it and clear the air, but we do not start a brick wall with one another over daily mistakes.

The other scenario for forgiving is when we have allowed years of un-forgiveness to accumulate within a current relationship or we have an accumulation of hurts from others stemming from our childhood or our past. When we don't deal quickly with daily hurts and offenses, they grow into walls. Perhaps we are in a relationship with a spouse who is neglectful and self-centered. Maybe we've tried to talk about our needs, but after many years of hurts, resentment has built up. We can choose to forgive or we can choose to stay miserable. Maybe a spouse has had an affair. They repented and have tried to regain trust, but the other person holds a grudge, refusing to truly forgive. Again there is a choice to forgive or feel miserable. True forgiveness is needed.

Childhood wounds affect all of us. As we looked at earlier in the chapter on Grace and Union, devotion on Hebrews 12:10-11, those wounds cause dents in our souls that lead us to believe lies about ourselves, which then causes us to act in ways that God does not intend. A father may have been absent, a mother may have been sick and unavailable emotionally, a sibling may have abused us, friends may have been cruel on the playground or death may have taken someone we loved. Not only do these wounds need to be healed by Jesus, we need to forgive the offender after we have processed the wound and the feelings connected to it. In any of these scenarios, we grant forgiveness the same way, but the ways in which we continue to relate to those who have hurt us may be different.

Application: Do you forgive others fairly quickly when "everyday" conflict arises or do you hold a grudge and retaliate? Do you have old wounds that you need to let Jesus heal so that you can truly forgive your offenders? Take time to consider what Jesus would have you do next.

GRANTING FORGIVENESS

"The LORD is gracious and merciful; Slow to anger and great in loving-kindness." Psalm 145:8

As we consider the facets of granting forgiveness, we might discover that we need to forgive ourselves or even God. We can be very angry at God when we begin to really look at and deal with how much we were hurt growing up and/or how neglected we were emotionally. It's common to blame God and be angry at Him for losses such as divorce or the death of a loved one. Of course God does not need or require any forgiveness from us, but sometimes after difficult situations have happened, we find that we are angry at Him and need to forgive Him. As this verse says, God can handle us being angry at Him and regardless of what we were taught about Him growing up, He's not waiting to throw a bolt of lightning at our heads.

I learned that God could handle my anger when our family was living by faith financially. We had to drive old vans and cars for which we could pay cash, and I cannot tell you how many times our vehicles broke down on an interstate or at home. One friend said he was tired of picking us up around town. After years of broken-down cars and in the midst of another, I was kneeling by my bed screaming at God. "I hate you! No wonder you have no friends. Look how you treat the ones who love You the most!!" I pounded my fists on the mattress in frustration, waiting on the lightening to come down from the sky.

That day was a breakthrough in intimacy for me. Not only did I not get struck by lightning, I found closeness to God that was new and wonderful. He loved me just the same when I was angry and frustrated with Him—

total honesty did not faze Him at all. I would never walk on eggshells with Him again. Freedom flooded my soul.

> ***Application:*** Have you ever admitted to yourself or someone else that you were angry at God? It's okay; He can handle it. Tell Him exactly how you feel—exactly. He loves honesty and loves you deeply.

"Thus says the LORD, 'Restrain your voice from weeping, And your eyes from tears; For your work shall be rewarded,' declares the LORD. . ." Jeremiah 31:16

Through the years I've talked with many people who need to forgive themselves because they are carrying guilt for past sins and mistakes, or even just foolish choices. Jeremiah tells us to let go of sorrow and regret and move forward. Jesus forgave us 2000 years ago, but when we haven't received the forgiveness, sometimes it means we need to forgive ourselves. One of the main things for which I've had to forgive myself is parenting failures. While rearing my children, I wish I could have known what I know now. Don't we all! Every good parent fails—they have to or their children would not need Jesus. The intellect tells us that we can only do what we know to do at the time, but good parents wish they could have done more and done it differently. Other regrets come if we're the spouse who had an affair and we've been forgiven and restored. Or we made career choices long ago that we wish we could do over. Regret is part of life, but carrying false guilt destroys our joy and peace. It's good to forgive ourselves and release those unnecessary burdens of guilt and condemnation.

> ***Application:*** Is there a place that you need to forgive yourself or even God? What regrets do you need to let go of and give to Him? Are

you certain that God can handle you being upset with Him? He knows it anyway. Be completely honest with the One who knows you best.

"**And so as those who have been chosen of God, holy and beloved, put on a heart of compassion, kindness, humility, gentleness and patience, bearing with one another and forgiving each other whoever has a complaint against anyone, just as the Lord forgave you, so also should you.**" Colossians 3:12-13

Paul tells us in this verse from Colossians, as he does in Ephesians 4:32 that we are to forgive others because we have been forgiven. Paul reminds us that we are chosen, holy, and beloved which moves us to treat others with compassion and kindness, humbly allowing Jesus' life to flow through us as His does to us.

There are times when we're ready to forgive another person, but we might need counsel or help from a third party to either discuss issues with the offender or be able to forgive them and let it go if we're unable to discuss it with them. Either alone with God or with a trusted friend, here we can see a good method for forgiving.

An effective way to grant forgiveness:

Take some time to pray through whether you need to let the other person know how they have hurt you. Many times this is not a wise or possible thing to do. When abuse has been part of your hurt, it may not be safe to confront the abuser or the offender. The offender may not be available. I also caution people not to forgive too soon. We may find that we have not processed the pain from abuse and neglect. If that is the case, take that step first with a Christ-centered counselor who understands emotional healing.

If you need to forgive someone for an accumulation of hurts, take some time to sit down and make a list of the hurts and wounds. You will *not* show this to the person you are going to forgive, even if they could be available. It can be written as a letter to that person. You will *not* mail or send the letter. Let yourself feel the hurt if you have not acknowledged that and felt it. It may help you to remember the hurts if you go back through picture albums.

When you have made your list, allowed yourself to feel the hurt, and are ready to forgive, get with a trusted friend or counselor in a private place. Place an empty chair in front of you. If it helps, you can put a picture of the person in this chair.

Read your list or letter aloud, or simply talk aloud, to the person as if he or she were there in the chair. Tell them all the hurts and wounds they have done to you. Get it all out. Cry or show anger. Your friend is there for support and accountability.

When you finish getting everything out, say to the "person" in the chair, "I forgive you, (their name). I will no longer hold these things against you. I release you for my good as well as yours." As you do this, you will sense that you have laid aside your pride and humbled yourself to grant them forgiveness. This is a very important step and will make a difference in your future relationships and your ability to practice daily forgiveness.

Have your friend or counselor close in prayer.

Choosing to forgive someone for hurting us frees us from bitterness and holding a grudge against this person. Forgiving releases us from all the energy we've had tied up and unavailable to us by holding on to un-forgiveness. It's common to feel lighter and find that we have more energy for living life.

Application: Are you already thinking of someone to whom you need to write a letter and put in the chair? Follow through with your intent. Ask someone, a trusted friend or counselor, to help you. You will regain lost energy that was sapping your strength.

"A peaceful heart leads to a healthy body; jealousy is like cancer in the bones." Proverbs 14:30 New Living Translation

As we've looked at granting forgiveness, we've seen a continual theme in the Scriptures—that forgiving others is first for our own benefit. Though this verse uses the word "jealousy" it's easy to realize that jealousy, envy, pride, and/or hatred are often the underlying symptoms that we need to forgive someone who has hurt us. The book of Proverbs is full of verses that encourage us to walk in God's ways—ways that bring peace and health.

Forgiveness is one of God's ways that brings peace and health. We saw in the chair exercise that the other person does not need to be present for us to forgive. He or she does not have to even know that we are forgiving them if the relationship is such that the incident cannot be discussed. When we forgive, we're doing it for ourselves, not for the other person—un-forgiveness affects our health and well being. Forgiving sets us free and helps us avoid a root of bitterness. (Hebrews 12:15) It does *not* mean that we condone in any way what the person has done to us. It does *not* mean that we totally forget what they did. But what it does mean is that the offense becomes less intrusive and less sharp in our mind. It also means that now we have given up the right to hold it against them. This has nothing to do with confronting the person, nor does it mean we will have a close relationship with them if they are some kind of danger to us.

Application: Consider these truths about forgiveness as you go about your day. Forgiveness is for your benefit, for your heath and your peace of mind regardless of what the other person does.

Keeping the account at zero:

After truly forgiving someone it's like wiping the slate clean. If we are in a normal relationship with this person, from that point on, we keep their account at zero by continuing to forgive as we go. This is the way to avoid building walls. If there is a person to whom we need to grant forgiveness but we're no longer in a relationship with them because of safety issues, divorce or death, we can still forgive them. We continue to keep the account at zero should other memories surface, though we may never be able to discuss anything with that person or even see them. We choose to keep their account at zero, not allowing offenses to pile up un-forgiven.

Forgiving is our choice and we are doing it for ourselves no matter what the other person knows or does. The slate is now clean and their account is zero. That means that we do not keep a running log of offenses in our mind. Some incidences might be discussed and worked out, but others will just be forgiven. Keeping accounts at zero will be very beneficial in normal, everyday type relationships because humility, which enhances any relationship, is a byproduct of being a forgiving person. As we forgive, walls that hinder intimacy come tumbling down when they no longer have the mortar of anger, pride, bitterness, and hate holding them together. As we continue to keep accounts at zero, there will be no bricks to begin a new wall. Lack of defensive walls will increase intimacy. A forgiving heart is a clear path to intimacy with Jesus as well.

Application: Have you wiped the slate clean about someone in the past but let a few little bumps come back into your heart towards their account? Tear down the new walls or remove the few bricks and get their account back to zero.

RECEIVING FORGIVENESS

"If we confess our sins, He is faithful and righteous to forgive us our sins and to cleanse us from all unrighteousness". I John 1: 9

Let's look now at our second aspect of forgiveness, that of receiving forgiveness. The major problem here seems to come from an inability to receive our forgiveness from God even though He has done everything to make it possible. People who have not received Christ as their Savior often find it difficult to believe that they can be forgiven for their sins simply by receiving the gift of salvation. They may feel that they need to "clean themselves up" first; they feel unworthy of forgiveness. Grace is not about being worthy; grace is a gift to be received.

Even after becoming a Christian, many people who received that initial forgiveness for their sins of the past find it difficult to receive forgiveness for things they have done as a Christian. As we have looked at already, it's easy to beat up on ourselves and we can carry tremendous, unnecessary guilt. Much of this kind of guilt comes from a lack of understanding about the finished work of Christ on the Cross, the significance of His resurrection, and how faith fits into our walk with Him. Let's look briefly at some ways to help us receive forgiveness and the freedom that comes with it.

Our verse in I John tells us that if we confess our sins, God is faithful and just to forgive us our sins. This verse can be applied to both before and after receiving Christ. Knowing what the word "confess" means can be very helpful. Confess means to "say the same thing as," "to agree with." Though it's somewhat of a lost idea in our society today, it's much the same as "taking responsibility for." God desires us to agree with Him about what we did—no more, no less. This leaves no room for carrying guilt or beating up on ourselves. We confess; He forgives. What generally happens is that we do not *feel* forgiven and thus go by that feeling rather than God's words. This is where faith comes in. In order to help us know we have received forgiveness, we can say "Thank You that I'm forgiven." Then we must let go of the guilt, stop stirring the bad memory of our sin, believe God and stand on the truth. Otherwise it's not faith. (Romans 14:23)

Sometimes it's necessary to stand on that truth, repeating the truth to ourselves many times until the guilt feelings are gone. We can exercise faith also by connecting with Jesus or another person who can help us with the truth so that we might "feel forgiven." Perceiving Jesus' presence in past experiences that feed guilt will help us when we struggle to receive our forgiveness.

As we continue to stand on the truth that we are forgiven and do what we can to truly believe it, it becomes evident to us that God is "faithful and just to forgive us." This means that He can be trusted; it is part of His character to keep His word. We can know that God is fair and exact about His promises concerning what Christ did on the Cross to make it possible for us to be forgiven.

Another idea that might help us receive forgiveness is to realize that when Christ died He died for all sins past, present and future. Our sins were all future when He died 2000 years ago. You might wonder then, "Why even confess if we've already been forgiven?" We confess, receive and thank Him by faith in order for it to be real in our experience; we must *receive* what He has done, both for salvation *and* for walking the journey.

Application: Are you still carrying guilt over a past sin? All your sins are forgiven. Talk to Jesus about anything you are still carrying guilt about. Ask Him where He was when you did the sin. You will be pleasantly surprised at His answer and His attitude towards you. Talk to Him until you can wholly receive your forgiveness.

"But He gives a greater grace. Therefore it says, 'God is opposed to the proud but gives grace to the humble.'" James 4:6

"Humble yourselves in the presence of the Lord and He will exalt you." James 4: 10

"If possible, so far as it depends on you, be at peace with all men."Romans 12:18

James and Paul, the writers here, assure us that humility is one of the true paths to intimacy with Christ and others. Humility comes before receiving, granting or seeking forgiveness. It is impossible to grant, receive or seek forgiveness with an attitude of pride. We grant forgiveness because we are forgiven. We forgive because we want to keep or restore close relationships.

Webster defines the word "humble" as, "having or showing a consciousness of one's defects or shortcomings; not proud; not self assertive; modest." "Proud," the opposite of humble, means, "having or showing an overwhelming opinion of oneself; arrogant; haughty." I think we all know when a person is seeking or granting a sincere apology. God will give us grace to receive, to grant or to seek forgiveness when we do it with humility.

Having humility and receiving forgiveness prevent us from beating up on ourselves. We confess the wrong, thank God that we are forgiven and go on. Pride may creep in and tell us we need to punish ourselves, but if we do not receive what Christ has done for that sin or mistake, we diminish what He did. (I Corinthians 15:14) What He did was sufficient. If we feel regret or the sin or mistake comes up again in our minds, we stand on the Truth of Christ's work that we are a forgiven person. If someone we have forgiven blows it again, we do the same with them. We allow no room for bricks to begin a new wall. If a person offends us, as Paul says in the Romans verse, be at peace as best we can, doing what is in *our* power to help the situation. Stir in that necessary ingredient of humility to bring healing and restoration to relationships.

Application: Do you struggle with humbling yourself to seek, grant or receive forgiveness? Do you sometimes feel you need to punish yourself when you mess up? Talk to Jesus about the completeness of

His work on the Cross and let Him reassure you that you are a forgiven person.

SEEKING FORGIVENESS

"If therefore you are presenting your offering at the altar and there remember that your brother has something against you, leave your offering there before the altar and go your way. . ."
Matthew 5: 23

The third aspect of forgiveness fits like a glove here with receiving and granting forgiveness, and again shows us the necessity of humility. As a habit of daily living, humbly seeking forgiveness can smooth and enhance relationships, bringing us back to joy with one another and preventing walls between us. Jesus tells us here in Matthew to seek forgiveness whenever we know someone has something against us. Letting it stew will affect our worship and fellowship. He says to be reconciled as soon as possible. Let's look at a way to reconcile quickly and sincerely.

Years ago, I learned this method of asking forgiveness that I cannot say enough about. It draws a line that helps us to know whether or not we are asking with humility. Whomever we are asking knows the difference, also.

Traditionally most people who want to make amends with another simply say, "I apologize" or "I'm sorry." The traditional response from the offended person is usually something along the lines of, "Oh, that's okay." There are several things wrong with this approach.

Saying that something worthy of an apology is okay is really a lie. It was not okay. Hearing, "I'm sorry," often leaves the offended person with few other choices as a response. Silence would be one other choice. The offender has not actually sought forgiveness. When the offended person has to be silent or say, "It's okay," that makes it easier to set a brick in place for that wall we talked about earlier.

> ***Application:*** How do you feel when someone just says, "I'm sorry," or you think their apology is not sincere? Do you find yourself saying that it's okay when it isn't? Talk to Jesus about your feelings.

". . . first be reconciled to your bother and them come and present your offering." Matthew 5:25

I think there is a much better way to seek forgiveness that leaves the offended person with three choices for responding without saying that the offense was okay. This method requires the offender to humble him or herself, confess the wrong and ask a question to which the other can answer. Just as in First John 1:9 the offender's confession will be to agree that there was a wrong by saying something like, "I was wrong to _____." Then comes the essential question—"Will you forgive me?" Now the offended one has the choice to say, "Yes, I forgive you," No, I don't forgive you," or "I'm not ready to forgive you." The offender has done his or her part and now it is up to the offended person to decide when and if he will forgive. If the other person is not ready, then the offender can say, "I hope you will be able to forgive me. If you want to talk more, I'll be available." It's fine to allow the offended one room to process and come to the point of granting forgiveness later. With some offenses it's better for the offender not to hurry and seek forgiveness if he or she is trying to salve his or her own guilt in order to feel better. Asking forgiveness is not a band-aid.

All these years that I've practiced this method or taught it to others, it has been very common when going to apologize to feel that prick of pride that wants to say, "I'm sorry," instead of, "I was wrong, will you forgive me." It definitely takes humility to do the latter. I know a mother who has taught her children to ask the humble question and when they just say, "I'm sorry" to her, she doesn't answer. Sometimes it takes the children three or four times before they say, "Will you forgive me?" Then she can answer, "Of course."

Application: I highly encourage you to consider this method of seeking forgiveness and make it a part of your life. When you have to say you are wrong and ask the question, laugh at yourself when you feel that prick of pride that wants to just say, "I'm sorry."

"Be angry and do not sin." Ephesians 4:26a

This verse is not usually one that is used about forgiveness, but in talking to deeply wounded people over the years, I realized that no one should be made to feel guilty or pressured about hurrying to forgive. With help we can feel anger that needs to be felt and not sin with it by hurting someone else. If someone has repressed or denied their emotions, they may need time to recognize and feel anger, sadness, fear or other feelings connected to the offenses. Forgiveness must not be a band-aid or a quick fix. It can take time for a person to come to a place of forgiveness. There are situations when one may not be able to confront an offender, but with love and help from God and a safe person, it is possible to forgive by faith.

Application: Are you someone who needs to realize how badly you were hurt and allow yourself to feel it? Have you been told to forgive too quickly? Get with a safe person or counselor who can help you forgive when the timing is right.

"And be kind one to another, tender hearted, forgiving one another, just as God in Christ has also forgiven you." Ephesians 4:32

Seeking, granting and receiving forgiveness are vital and key to intimacy with God and others, good health, and a good life. When all three aspects of forgiveness are incorporated as a part of daily interactions, the dynamics of those relationships will benefit greatly as people find it easier to return to joy when relationship ruptures occur. God has done all that is necessary for our forgiveness from Him. He desires us to grant the same to others. We seek, grant and receive forgiveness every day as a choice so that we do not have to carry guilt, shame, bitterness or pride. Forgiving eliminates much of our baggage from the past, resets current relationships with more intimacy, and paves the way for daily harmony. Like faith, hope and love, forgiveness is an important ingredient for intimacy with Christ.

INTIMACY THROUGH REST AND PEACE

We will look at this chapter as three sections: Rest with God, Rest with circumstances, and Rest with others.

REST AND PEACE IN RELATIONSHIP WITH GOD

"Rest in the Lord and wait patiently for Him." Psalm 37:7

"Return to your rest, O my soul, for the Lord has dealt bountifully with you."Psalm116:7

All through the Scriptures we are told to rest. What exactly does it mean to rest? What keeps us from experiencing 'rest for our souls' about which this verse speaks? How do we get to a place of rest? What does it feel like when I am not resting?

In my experience, I realize I'm not resting when I feel myself worrying and fretting. What's really going on is I'm not trusting God. He is the source and center of rest. If fretting continues, it turns into stress. Worry, stress, and fretting are so difficult to handle and let go of—and so easy to fall into. They make our stomachs churn and our heads ache and our bodies sick—they are the opposite of rest and peace. God made us to live in joy and peace; in intimacy with Him surrounded by inner peace that calms and replaces worry and stress. So how do we get to this place of rest? I think we can find some answers as we look at these three aspects of rest—rest in relation to God, rest in our circumstances, and rest with other people.

When we are worrying and fretting, many times it's because we believe that we can control God, our circumstances, and other people. Trying to control does not bring rest. I know because I used to be a chronic co-dependent who believed I could make my circumstances better by

154

loving and serving. I mistakenly believed I could get the outcome I wanted by loving enough or serving diligently. I was very tired from confusing God's agapè love and co-dependent love. I found help as Dr. Wilder helped me see the difference:

Co-dependency is trying to save the other person from their pain by trying to fix their pain. Co-dependents enable another person to avoid their pain or the co-dependent removes the other's pain by feeling their pain for them.

Agapè love means we sit with the other person in the pain or use 'tough love' when toughness is necessary.

Dr. Wilder continues: "Taking away suffering that belongs to someone else is not love, if it keeps that person from learning from his or her mistakes. When pain is shared it teaches that when necessary, pain can be endured."[65]

As I took hold of these truths, I began to realize when I was feeling another's pain for them. I recognized that I was not experiencing that inner rest and peace that comes from trusting God. I was trying to control something that was not mine to control—and it was not even possible to control. Learning to love with God's love and trust Him with outcomes helped me stop being co-dependent with others and "find rest for my soul."

Application: Do you realize when you're not resting and trusting God because you are "feeling someone else's feelings" for them so they don't have to feel anything negative? Are you exhausted yet from trying to get a certain outcome from certain situations? You will find rest when you realize that there are many things you cannot control.

---

[65] E. James Wilder, *Red Dragon Cast Down*, Chose Books, Grand Rapids, MI 49516, 1999, paraphrased page 176

"There remains therefore a Sabbath rest for the people of God. For the one who has entered His rest has himself also rested from his works; as God did from His. Let us therefore be diligent to enter that rest, lest anyone fall through following the same example of disobedience. " Hebrews 4: 10-11

Trying to control and feel others' emotions is far from rest. Keeping busy was another way that I tried to keep my own emotions at bay and feel good about myself.   I hoped it would bring rest. It was not until I met Laurie Hills, a lovely lady who was friends with Dan Stone and Norman Grubb that I began to understand resting in the Lord. Laurie pointed out that verse eleven here says we have to "be diligent to enter God's rest." The King James Version translates "diligent" as "labor."   We have to "labor to enter rest." Using "labor" and "rest" in the same sentence sounds contradictory. God's rest is available, but like other things that are already true, we have to "take" that they are true. (See the chapter on Grace and Union, devotion Ephesians 1:3-5)

As we continue to take something that is already true in God's eyes, there comes a point at which the Holy Spirit reveals to our hearts that it really is true. At the beginning, we are "laboring," in a sense, to say the truth when it does not *feel* true. Believing against our feelings can feel like work, but in reality, we are taking what *is* true until the Spirit makes it real in our experience. After the Spirit reveals it to our heart, we know that we know that we know. Knowing is a spirit function, not an intellectual or emotional function.

After learning who I was in Christ and knowing I was accepted by Him, I found some rest from thinking I had to do everything perfectly to be okay. I did not have to stay busy to avoid looking at the places I could not perform and get acceptance. I "took" that there was a Sabbath rest for me and that I was okay even when I failed to perform perfectly. After the Spirit made this real to me and calmed my drive to be perfect, I could rest better inside.

Rest comes when, instead of striving to please God by trying to meet our own needs through performing perfectly or by getting our own way, we practice diligence in taking what is true of us in the Spirit and as we experience Jesus' presence. I will always be the type of person who likes to be busy, but my busyness now is from a different place inside. I do what I want to do and the reason is out of love. I know that I am loved by Jesus and I don't have to do things for people in order for them to "like" and accept me. When I feel stressful thoughts, I turn to Jesus who is our Rest. Life is too short to spend it hurrying and scurrying because we feel unloved.

> *Application:* Rest is the opposite of stress and the path to rest begins in your mind. Begin to notice when you feel that whirring in your mind or churning in your stomach. Turn to Jesus and claim that He has made it possible for you to rest. He has everything in His hands. He is big enough to take care of you and your circumstances. Take the truths that bring rest until God's rest takes you.

"But the fruit of the Spirit is love, joy, peace, patience, kindness, goodness, faithfulness, gentleness, self-control; against such things there is no law." (Galatians 5:22-23)

"For He Himself is our peace, who made both groups into one, and broke down the barrier of the dividing wall." Ephesians 2:14

"And His name shall be called Wonderful Counselor, Mighty God, Eternal Father, Prince of Peace." Isaiah 9:6c

In the verses from Galatians, we can see another aspect of rest and peace. The first part of this Galatians passage is often misquoted and misunderstood. Most frequently it's quoted as "the fruits of the Spirit are." When looked at that way where "fruit" is plural, the characteristics become something for which we have to strive. It's as if the fruits are in a vending machine and we have to go get one when we need it—pull a lever and that "fruit" will come out. We often forget to go get one and end up acting out the opposite characteristic. I would like to propose that "fruit" is singular for a reason. Fruit is singular because we see in the Ephesians and Isaiah verses above, the "fruit," (peace, for example) is a person—Jesus Himself. As our perspective changes, we can see that all of the characteristics in Galatians 5:22-23 are who Jesus is. He is our love, our joy, our peace, our patience (verse 22); our gentleness, our self-control (verse 23). We see that "Jesus is" in the Ephesians and Isaiah verses as well.

What a liberating truth—we don't need a vending machine—we have the whole package within us! As believers in Christ, Jesus is our life, our all. When we need patience, we don't pray, "O Lord, give me patience." By faith we say, "Lord, I am feeling impatient right now, but You are my patience." When we feel anxious, we can say, "Lord, I need You to be my peace right here so I won't worry and fret. Thank You." Then we proceed, expecting Him to live through us. *He* is the fruit of the Spirit. In the chapter on Prayer and Communion we will look at some other ways to pray when we need the "fruit."

Application: As you think about the fruit of the Spirit, ask Jesus to live through you in the places you struggle rather than asking Him *for* that fruit. If you have a hard time speaking that He is your peace, for example, try the tapping exercise from the devotion on Colossians 3:15, further on in this chapter, to get your relational circuits back on. After you tap your chest, you may need to continue with something like, "I'm feeling anxious here, Lord, what do You want me to know about this?" There is more on that in the Matthew 7:7 devotion right after Colossians 3:15. Keep turning to Jesus.

REST AND PEACE IN CIRCUMSTANCES

"Come unto Me you who are weary and heavy-laden and I will give you rest. Take My yoke upon you, and learn from Me, for I am gentle and humble in heart: and you shall find rest for your souls. For My yoke is easy and My load is light." Matthew 11:28-30

In this passage, Jesus uses a word picture that His listeners would have understood, but in our day, about the only example we have of a "yoke" is pictures we've seen in movies or books. It's important to realize that a yoke is made for two, not one. I suppose someone could plow with an ox on one side, but it seems very unlikely. The empty yoke would slump over and drag the ground. Jesus is telling us here that He is the Other in the yoke. That's why it's easy and light. He does the work. We co-operate. Two in a yoke cannot go different directions; they have to work together. Just imagine what it would be like if each ox tried to pull a plow or a wagon in his one direction within the yoke. He could pull as hard as possible, wear himself out, and get nowhere.

Our compassionate Master knows that living without Him is way too much for us alone and that it will not work. That's why there is a yoke. The yoke might feel funny, or constricting when the Farmer snaps it in place over our shoulders, yet what a joy, what a relief when the Other is snapped into the yoke beside us. The burden suddenly becomes "easy" and "light."

Rest is not necessarily a physical thing. For me, rest is mostly in my mind, which transfers to the physical. Stress comes when our minds whir and worry. Just today thinking about this book, my mind started to stir and leap from one idea or verse to another. After many years of practice, it's easier to notice, and immediately I said to Jesus, "Slow me down. I don't have to remember all these verses and ideas that go through my mind like a river. You will tell me, guide me and remind me." That is rest.

When we finally get weary of trying to live in our own strength, all alone in that heavy yoke, the invitation for rest is always there. We take the yoke to learn from Him, to draw on His strength and power, to be the other half of what He's up to, not to boss Him around with our whining and demanding. What we learn of Him is that He is patient and kind and loving, and that He "can do nothing of Himself, unless it is something He sees the Father doing." (John 5:19) Jesus wants us to learn to follow Him the way He followed the Father; He wants us to let Him live through us the way the Father lived through Him.

> *Application:* Where do you need to find rest and share the yoke with Jesus? Is it financially; family; relationships; career? What thoughts do you stir that only take away your joy and rest? Take your stressful thoughts and worries to the Master who never intended for you to carry burdens that are His to carry.

"The steadfast of mind Thou will keep in perfect peace because he trusts in Thee." Isaiah 26:3

"Be anxious for nothing, but in everything by prayer and supplication with thanksgiving, let your request be made known to God. And the peace of God which surpasses all comprehension shall guard your heart and your minds in Christ Jesus." Philippians 4:6-7

Just as heavy burdens pull us down, anxiety destroys our peace. We've already looked at the concept of "setting your mind" in our devotion on Colossians 3:2 in the Grace and Union chapter as one path to peace and freedom. In the Isaiah verse above, we see "steadfast of mind" as a way to peace. Webster tells us that "steadfast" means "constant, steady, and firmly fixed." A person whose mind is steadfastly (constantly) focused on God will be able to trust Him and experience peace. Upon first look, we could feel like we somehow have to always be thinking about God; that every second must be focused on Him. In truth, that's impossible to do with any topic. It seems to me the idea is more about learning to turn to Him for everything that comes up—gratitude for all He gives and does; comfort for trials and hurts; petitions for needs. The constancy and steadiness are an enveloping sense that He is real and involved in every area of our lives whether we are consciously thinking of Him every second.

When we feel anxious about circumstances, our emotions may not feel peaceful, but deep inside there can be a surety that God is in control. A couple of years ago I had to move from a home I dearly loved to another house. My emotions were anything but peaceful and restful. What kept me going was steadfastly focusing on God in spite of my strong feelings. I had to remind myself, or be reminded, of His goodness and sovereignty. Anabel Gillham's envelope story from the chapter on Suffering and Trials, devotion John 14:20 reminded me that nothing can come into my life if it does not come through God and Jesus first, and when a circumstance gets to me, "it finds me filled with Jesus."[66] I kept that truth in mind.

Paul tells us in the Philippians verse, when circumstances make us anxious, not to worry at all. This doesn't mean that we will never feel anxious, just that we can turn to God and listen to Him and expect Him to respond with peace that is more than we can understand. (In the chapter on Feelings and Appearances we will look closely at how to listen to God and hear His voice.) We are able to turn to God in our anxiety because of Jesus. Focusing on Jesus and turning to Him when we feel anxious or worried builds intimacy. Remember in the chapter on Grace and Union, devotion I Corinthians 6:17 where we talked about Laurie Hill's fist-in-hand illustration? Anxious thoughts and circumstances "pull" us to turn out from our union with Christ; turning back to Jesus and steadfastly focusing on Him with prayer and supplication produces peace and rest in our hearts regardless of our emotions. Over and over and over we are seeing that the path to intimacy is to turn to Jesus and trust Him.

My friend, Scott Sellmann, who owns his own business, has a good illustration of how it feels to have emotional pressure during anxious

---

[66] Anabel Gillham, *The Confident Woman*, 1993, Harvest House Publishers, Eugene, OR 97402, page 95

circumstances while we are trying at the same time to steadfastly focus on Jesus. Scott calls his illustration "The Funnel:"

> "Being anxious for nothing" and keeping a "steadfast mind" on God sometimes sounds easier than it actually is. I see the struggle like a funnel. Say at the top of the funnel is where you have a little anxiety because you're having a slower week with work coming in, and you know it's going to affect the finances some. But you are able to say, "I know God's in control," and rest in that. But then a second week of slower work rolls around (now you're in the middle of the funnel), and the pressure is increasing, and you again have to choose, but now it's harder, more pressurized, but you remember all of the times when God has come through and so you come back to peace. But then the third week in a row comes around, and you're in the bottom of the funnel, extreme pressure, extreme emotions and this time it's really hard to come to peace and rest. Focusing on Jesus and not your emotions or circumstances is easier or harder depending on where you are in the funnel.

__Application:__ Scott's funnel might make it easier for you to give yourself grace under pressure. When you feel anxious, turn to Jesus and make Him your focus as much as possible. Ask Him what He wants you to know about the pressure in the funnel.

"And let the peace of Christ rule in your hearts. . ." Colossians 3:15

Noticing when we lack peace "ruling our hearts" is like a referee at a sporting event. The lack of peace signals that something is off in our lives. What we need is to sense God's presence when we feel anxious. Knowing

He is with us is the best path to calming down. His presence will helps us rest, but it's not always easy to find Him in the middle of being upset. When we get into the bottom of the funnel of stress that takes away our peace, it can help to do some physical exercises that help us calm. In our brains there are relational circuits that have to be "turned on" in order for us to relate to others. They need to be on to relate to God as well. Simply tapping your fingers back and forth on each side of your chest while taking a deep breath will calm your anxious brain and turn your brain's "relational circuits" back on.[67] As you expel the deep breath say, "Whenever I am afraid I will trust in You, O LORD." (Psalm 56:3 KJV) Repeat the exercise a couple of times. As your brain and body calm, it will be easier to sense God's presence and hear His voice.

Application: At first this simple exercise may seem silly to you, but I encourage you to try it any time you feel anxious and lose your peace. There are two nerves that run through your body on each side of the sternum from your chest down. Tapping back and forth on each of the two nerves calms and "resets" your brain. This exercise is easy to do inconspicuously even in public and can be done with one hand while driving. Give it a try. Share it with your family so that everyone can remind each other an easy way to calm.

---

[67] Exercise taken from *Belonging Facilitator Workbook*, Ed Khouri, E. James Wilder, Shepherd's House Inc. P.O. Box 40096, Pasadena, CA, 91114, page 59; www.thrivingrecovery.org

"Ask, and it shall be given to you; seek, and you shall find; knock, and it shall be opened to you." Matthew 7:7

"But if any of you lacks wisdom, let him ask of God who gives to all men generously and without reproach, and it will be given to him. But let him ask in faith without any doubting, for the one who doubts is like the surf of the sea driven and tossed by the wind." James 1:5

God is eager to relate to us and show us His ways. When we feel lost about a situation or a decision, He wants to give us His wisdom. Sometimes when we turn to God to get answers, they don't come as quickly as we would like. James is encouraging us to believe God's promise without doubting. That can be difficult. Depending on the situation about which we're asking God, we may feel like we are being tossed in the surf by a raging sea, our thoughts scattered, making it hard to know how to handle what is going on. In their booklet, *Share Immanuel*, Dr. Wilder and Chris Coursey have come up with some suggestions that can help us hear God.

In order to calm our scattered thoughts, we can turn our minds to something we appreciate. It does not have to be something "spiritual," just something that makes us breathe a sigh and feel warm and safe. Beaches, babies sleeping, warm blankets, and nature are all examples of things that we can appreciate and help us calm. When we are calm, we can ask Jesus some questions and sit quietly to hear His answers:

"What do you want me to know about this _____?"

"What is Your perspective on what I am going through or feeling?"

"Where are You right now in this trial?"

"Where were you when _____ happened?"[68]

---

[68] More information on these questions and other helps during unrest and loss of peace, may be found in the *Share Immanuel* booklet by E. James Wilder and Christ Coursey at www.lifemodel.org or www.thrivetoday.org As I lead small

As we learn to talk to Jesus and recognize His voice, we can have a dialogue with Him about whatever is bothering us. Like the verse above tells us, we can ask Him about anything. I have found that hearing what He has to say most often brings peace to my heart. All we have to do is ask. We will look more closely at this in the chapter on Prayer and Communion. For now, continue to note that the path to intimate rest and peace is through bringing our thoughts of anxiety, worry, doubts and fear to Jesus and hearing what He wants us to know about them.

> *Application:* If listening for God to answer you is a new concept, see the later chapter, *Feelings and Appearances—Barriers to Intimacy,* devotion II Corinthians 11:14 and devotion I Kings 19: 11-12. These two devotions will help you see how to distinguish God's voice from Satan's. In the chapter on Prayer and Communion, there will be more examples of "conversing" with Jesus.

"But each one is tempted when he is carried away and enticed by his own lust. Then when lust has conceived, it gives birth to sin. And when sin is accomplished, it brings forth death." James 1:14:15

A misunderstanding of temptation can cause us unrest. No one taught me growing up that temptation and sin are different. I believed that if I was tempted, I had sinned. I would beat up on myself and/or ask forgiveness for sinning when I had only been tempted. Confusing temptation and sin made for lots of unnecessary guilt and worry. When I understood that temptation was like a pull to sin, but I did not have to give in to the pull, it was easier to see what James is saying here. Dan Stone

---

groups, I am using several resources that are more in depth on this way to pray, in order to help others learn to "ask of God."

explains it very well in his book, *The Rest of the Gospel* by asking the question, "How does lust conceive?" Dan goes on to answer his question:

> Lust conceives through union. When you join yourself to it. When you decide, given the chance, you will do it. When do male and female produce a child? When they join themselves together. Life doesn't come out of a thought or a feeling. Life comes out of a choice. So until you make that choice (even if in your mind), until you join yourself to it, you haven't sinned yet.[69]

Dan's answer is similar to what Jesus told us in Matthew 5:28: "But I say to you that everyone who looks upon a woman to lust for her, has committed adultery with her already in his heart." Jesus was saying something like, "If you have decided in your heart, that given the chance you will do this, it is as if you have done it." The inner choice has been made and it's not just a thought or feeling. The difference in temptation and sin is the motive and choice. When we see the difference, we will be more easily drawn to intimacy with Jesus because we will not constantly think we are sinning and displeasing Him.

When I first understood that temptation was not a sin, it felt like I needed to hit my forehead and say, "Duh." Jesus was tempted and He never sinned, but for some reason I thought my bad feelings and thoughts made me bad. Feeling false shame does not make for intimacy with Christ. I gained much freedom when I learned to distinguish a temptation from the choice to give in to it.

In the chapter on Feelings and Appearances we will talk more about how thoughts and feelings affect our lives.

Application: Have you been feeling guilty when you feel a pull of temptation but do not give in to it? Notice the next time you feel that pull and do not take condemnation for the temptation. Do not give in and you won't sin. If you fail, God is waiting to forgive and restore.

---

[69] *The Rest of the Gospel, When the partial Gospel has worn you out*, One Press, Dallas Texas, page 196, paraphrased.

REST AND PEACE IN RELATIONSHIPS WITH OTHERS

". . . (Find) where the good way is and walk in it. And you shall find rest for your souls. Jeremiah 6:16.

Another facet of rest has to do with getting along well with other people. We looked at some differences in God's kind of love and co-dependent love in the first devotion of this chapter. Co-dependent love happens when we allow a person to step on our boundaries. Some boundary bashers get their way when we don't speak up or we disengage when they blow up. Other boundary bashers just retreat to avoid conflict. Neither blowing up or retreating brings rest. A growly person blows up like a bear to keep others from telling them they are wrong. They stop discussions with their anger. Other people retreat like a turtle for the same reason—to avoid being told there is a problem. Either way when we act out of co-dependency, we are not trusting God, we are not helping our relationships, nor are we finding rest.

Neither avoiding conflict by blowing up nor retreating to hide is God's kind of love. If we act a certain way—blowing up or retreating—to obtain an outcome, that is co-dependency. Looking for an outcome means we make our decisions based on trying to get another person to act the way we want them to act. That can be a subtle form of manipulation. The opposite is true of *agapè* love— God's kind of love. Agapè love does things because of our character or God's Spirit impels us. *Agapè* love is not related to success or probable responses; it's dependent only on the character of the one acting.

As I grew to understand the difference between loving someone because of Jesus living through me and trying to fix a circumstance or enabling someone to avoid pain, it became easier to rest.

> ***Application:*** Which kind of response do you tend to make when conflict arises—growly bear or hiding turtle? Neither is God's way, although our culture seems to think turtles are nicer than bears. Consider that both responses are a form of manipulation and talk to Jesus about better ways to respond. Do things out of your character as a loving person. You may have to find a place to practice coming out of your shell if you tend to be a turtle. If you tend to be a bear, you will need help and healing for your anger and fear.

"'For the Son of Man is Lord of the Sabbath.' And departing from there, He went into their synagogue. And behold, there was a man with a withered hand. And they questioned Him, saying, 'Is it lawful to heal on the Sabbath?'—In order that they might accuse Him. And He said to them, 'What man shall there be among you, who shall have one sheep, and if it falls into a pit on the Sabbath will he not take hold of it and lift it out?'" Matthew 12:8-11**

"'Of how much more value then is a man than a sheep! So then, it is lawful to do good on the Sabbath.' Then He said to the man, Stretch out your hand!' And he stretched it out and it was restored to normal, like the other." Matthew 12: 12-13**

Learning to walk in *agapè* love instead of co-dependency will upset people around us. Jesus upset people by telling them the truth and doing things that did not go along with their man-made rules, their ideas about how He should act, and their ideas of God's laws. As we see here, He healed people on the Sabbath. Earlier in Matthew 12 the disciples picked grain and ate the heads which was considered work. (Verse 1) He reminded the self-righteous people about King David eating the consecrated bread. (Verse 4)

Reading about Jesus upsetting people was one thing—learning to accept that I might have to learn to do it was another. Loving and serving some people in order to fix things was not working—and certainly was not bringing rest. As I talked to Dr. Wilder, he upset me with one of his truths: "Everyone is an upsetting person. You feel badly when you upset someone. You are trying *not* to be one, instead of accepting that you are a real upsetting person. Jesus was a very upsetting person—He upset lots of folks. He doesn't want to be with people who do all things right, but with people who are willing to admit they are upsetting. You lack peace about being an upsetting person."

This is a particular truth I am continuing to work on. I like to remember it when I know I have upset someone when it was necessary. I remember a time when I had to tell a roommate that I was selling my house. She got very upset. It was difficult to know that someone had to find another place to live because I was moving, but it was necessary. As a mentor I've had to tell people things they did not want to hear. When told something they don't want to hear, it's easy for people to try to hurt the messenger by getting defensive, getting upset, or attacking. The messenger has to stand firm and trust Jesus.

Telling someone something they need to hear, but don't want to hear, is different than when we hurt someone by blowing up or retreating. I remember a time when I was teaching at a Christian school, where I and some other teachers took a stand against a new policy that we thought was very unfair. We signed a student-led petition that wanted the administrators to change the new policy later, after the current seniors had graduated. With only two weeks of school left, we were told that if we said one word against the decision to keep the new policy, we would have to turn in our keys. I wanted to say something during the meeting in order to stand up for the students, but because it was the last two weeks of school, I kept my mouth shut. Even though it felt like I was going against my principles, I knew it would be easier for the students to take exams with me rather than with a new teacher or substitute. Needless to say, I was not invited back the next year and neither would I have accepted if invited. This was an organization much like what Jesus ran into in our verses here—leaders who thought only about rules and not about people.

Like the Pharisees, people get upset when confronted with their selfishness or self-righteousness. We upset our children when we discipline them for their good. There is a chance people will get upset when we talk about God. I want to learn to rest in the fact that I, and everyone else, am an upsetting person.

> ***Application:*** The next time you find yourself having to upset someone, try picturing Jesus as an upsetting person. When you know you have to stand up for truth rather than following a pharisaical rule, take courage and be willing to upset the religious people. Follow the Spirit and "do good."

"Bear one another's burden and thus fulfill the law of Christ."
Galatians 6: 2

"For each one shall bear his own load."Galatians 6: 5

These verses have helped me learn to rest by reminding me what is mine to carry and what is not. In verse two, *burden* in the Greek gives us a picture of a large boulder. When we have a boulder to carry, we need help from others. We look at this verse most times, and see what to do when someone is in need.

What if *you* are "the someone" in need? Painful losses such as the death of a loved one, a divorce or having cancer are "boulders" we sometimes have to carry where we need the support of a loving community. If we lose our job, we may need help from others to push through. Rearing a family takes support from others, as does going through the process of healing past wounds. All these are examples of burdens with which we will need help if we are going to rest in the Lord while they're going on.

In verse five, we see that in some instances we bear our own load. *Load* in the Greek gives us the picture of a backpack, something we're able to handle. Daily chores and activities are examples of our loads. We go about most days just living life and doing whatever mundane things that come along. We share the daily stuff with family, friends and co-workers, but most of the time we carry on without losing our peace. When backpacks become too hard to carry, when we have lost our peace and can't get back to joy, we call that depression. We are no longer at rest. Now our backpack has grown into a boulder and we need to ask for extra help.

As we go through our daily lives, taken in context, these verses tell us we need Jesus during both. As Galatians 5: 25 tells us, "If we live by the Spirit, let us also walk by the Spirit." Whether we are experiencing a boulder or a backpack, we need Jesus. We do not want to get into the thinking that says, "This is too small for God," or even, "This is too big for God." Jesus wants us to bring *everything* to Him.

Application: What are some boulders in your life? Do you have help or need to ask for help? Turn to Jesus, but get human help where it's needed. Do you have any backpacks you are whining about that are part of your daily load? Distinguish the two. Check to see if you need to change your attitude to one of gratitude. Jesus wants to know about all your boulders and loads.

"Rest in the Lord and wait patiently for Him." Psalm 37:7

Resting in the Lord is like a child sitting in his father's lap. The child feels safe and loved; he knows that the father will take care of all that comes his way. There are no burdens too big to carry; he needs only to trust the father. Sometimes the child will wander away to explore and go about his daily life, but in the back of his mind he knows the father's lap is there waiting. Trials and storms will come his way; temptations will pull, but rest can be found whenever he trusts the Father's strength, concern, sovereignty, and wisdom. *"Wait patiently,"* He says to us. *"I'm at work even when you cannot see what I'm doing. My main desire is intimacy with you regardless of your circumstances. Rest, My Beloved."*

INTIMACY THROUGH LOVE, JOY AND BONDING

"But God demonstrates His own love toward us, in that while we were yet sinners, Christ died for us." Romans 5:8

"For God so loved the world, that He gave His only begotten Son, that whoever believes in Him should not perish but have eternal life." John 3 16

Though love is a topic about which many entire books have been written, it's important for us to include love as a topic here. We will look at a scattering of verses that encourage us to love God, ourselves and others. We start with these two verses because what they say is the basis of all kinds of love. We are able to have intimacy with God and others because of God's great love that He demonstrated when He sent His Son to die for us. Without Christ we would not be able to love God and other people. I John 4:19 tells us, "We love because He first loved us." We walk with the God of the universe who loved us first, when we had nothing that made us deserve His love. He loved us just because we are. He did what was necessary to show us what His kind of love looks like. He lives in us to be the power we need to spread that kind of love to our world.

But as we all know, we don't always *feel loving* towards God or others. As we look at these verses and comments, it will be good to think back to what we saw in the Grace and Union chapter: Jesus lives in us, and He wants to live His life through us, in His power. In reading about love here, do not forget that love is a Person: Jesus Himself. When we don't feel loving, we can ask Jesus to love through us in His power. We can say something like, "Lord, right now I don't feel very loving towards my friend (spouse, child). I know that You are love and that You live in me. I believe that You love _____ through me, and I trust You to keep my words or actions from hurting them. Guide me in how to find a solution to this situation. Thank you, Lord."

Sometimes when we are upset with someone, it could be what we call a "trigger," that is, the upset is really about someone from our past and not the person in front of us. If what we are feeling about the person in front of us seems out of proportion to the circumstances that could be a sign we are triggered. We can ask Jesus to show us where it is coming from in our past relationships and let Him heal the old wound.[70]

Over the years after either praying for Jesus to love through me or getting a past wound healed, I've seen God change my feelings towards someone who seemed hard to love.

> *Application:* As you go about your day, think often about God's great love and how much He loves you and wants to interact with you no matter what is going on. If you run into a difficult situation with another person that calls for you to love them, remember that Jesus will love them through you if you ask.

"Love is patient, love is kind, and is not jealous; love does not brag and is not arrogant, does not act unbecomingly; it does not seek its own, is not provoked, does not take into account a wrong suffered, does not rejoice in unrighteousness but rejoices with the truth; bears all things, believes all things, hopes all things endures all things. Love never fails. . ." **I Corinthians 13:4-8**

---

[70] For more on triggers see my book, *Joy-Filled Relationships*, pages 149-152; and/or *Outsmarting Yourself* by Dr. Karl Lehman. www.kclehman.com Also go back to the devotion on James 1:5 in Rest and Peace.

The "love chapter" in I Corinthians 13 has likely had more words written about it than most other chapters in the Bible. These verses are often used in weddings as a pledge of what couples will try to do. It's important for us to realize that we cannot pull off this kind of love in our own strength. This is God's kind of love. He wants us to experience this kind of love from Him to us and then, through His power, let Him live out this kind of love to others. We might have to ask Jesus to love through us, but as we experience His love to us, it becomes easier to love ourselves and others. Sometimes we sum up this love chapter by saying, "We love unconditionally. We love regardless of behavior." I like to say we have "two windows of love" through which to look. Let's explore those two windows in the next two devotions.

Application: Which of the attributes of love speaks to you? These attributes are Jesus' character. Is there a place that you don't know Him as one of these? Is there a place you need to trust Him to live through you to someone else?

"A friend loves at all time." Proverbs 17: 17 a

"A new commandment I give to you, that you love one another, even as I have loved you, that you also love one another." John 13:34

There are basically two windows of love—conditional love and unconditional love. I want to focus on looking through the window of unconditional love, because we all know it can be a struggle to love unconditionally and authentically. One day after I renamed the windows—behavior and personhood—I found it easier to separate them and keep my focus on the window of unconditional love. If I looked through the window I was now calling "behavior," I was only able to love conditionally. If I looked through the other window, "personhood," I was able to love unconditionally. Separating someone's behavior from his or her personhood helped me to be able to look at myself and others as who we are rather than what we do.

Separating who we are from what we do is not an easy task. Our culture and society so emphasize performance that we are almost brainwashed into seeing others and ourselves through the window that makes evaluations based on behavior. What we believe is, "I'm bad if I do something bad. I'm good if I do something good." That would be the same as saying, "I'm a cat because I 'meow.'"

Being able to see a person's heart, who they are, requires a different window. Muddy smudges, such as judgment, blaming, rejection and contempt, cover the window of behavior, distorting our perception of others and interfering with our ability to show authentic love. Jesus, the Person who *is* unconditional love has to teach us how to stop looking through the muddy smudges, while teaching us how to look at people through the window of the heart, through their personhood. Knowing Jesus loves me unconditionally is one of the ways I experience intimacy with Him. It's easier to cuddle up closely to someone who loves me no matter what.[71]

> ***Application:*** Is there anyone whom you are evaluating based on their behavior? Ask Jesus what He wants you to know about that.

---

[71]From blog, *Two Windows of Love* at www.barbaramoon.wordpress.com

"And walk in love, just as Christ also loved you and gave Himself up for us. . ." Ephesians 5:2a

We are called to a lifestyle of looking at others through the window of God's kind of love. I remember two unmarried young people who moved in to live together. I spoke to them once about my feelings on the matter (of course they already knew my feelings) and then I loved them and related to them the same as if they were married. Without my condemnation or interference, I watched them work through what they needed to learn, grow tremendously from the experience and then get married. Condemning or rejecting them for their unwise behavior did not fit with what God was teaching me about the two windows.

During these events, I had some important goals. First and foremost, I did not want to lose the relationship with these young people. I wanted to see them through the window of personhood and love them for who they are—to keep the relationship and know that we would stay connected. It was my desire that, when, like the prodigal son, their journey brought them back to their true values, I would be one to whom they would come for support or help. I'm thankful to say that they did return and we've had joy in those relationships ever since.

Another goal in my heart was for these young people to truly know that they are loved unconditionally. They had heard it taught and knew the words. But it was one thing to tell them how loved they are and another for them to know it deeply in themselves. Being loved in spite of their behavior helped them experience that what they do is not who they are. Bad or unwise behavior does not make them bad or unwise. Years have now passed and they've been married a long time. Most of the time they look at each other through the personhood window showing evidence in their lives that these lessons of love were valuable and life changing. The lessons also brought them an added benefit—they know how to love others authentically.[72]

---

[72]See *Two Windows of Love* and *Learning Authentic/Unconditional Love* at www.barbaramoon.wordpress.com)

Application: Through which window do you look at those around you—a clear one of personhood and heart or a muddy window filled with judgment? Begin today to separate personhood and behavior and note the difference in how you react to those whose behavior is not perfect. Ask Jesus to fill you with God's kind of love.

"And you shall love the LORD your God with all your heart and with all your soul and with all your mind, and with all your strength. . ." Mark 12:30

"When some tricky scribes asked Jesus for the most important commandment, Mark tells us that Jesus answered with these words—to love God with all our beings. It seems to me that many of us could have a slight problem with this command. We are commanded to love God with all of our being, but if we don't know Him (remember "getting to know the ice" in the Faith chapter, devotion Hebrews 11:6a?) it will be very difficult to love Him and trust Him.

As we consider how much He loves us and all He has done, we will find it easier to draw near to Him. We might have to find healing for painful memories that cast a shadow over our Heavenly Father because of wrongs done by our earthly fathers or mothers. Fathers or mothers who did not love us well affect our view of God. Whatever it takes for healing and understanding will be worth whatever we have to go through to experience His love to us and ours to Him.

Application: Again you can see the importance of getting to know what God is really like so that you can love Him with all your being. Consider getting help for any painful wounds you may have from your past that hinder your love and intimacy with God.

". . . the second is this, you shall love your neighbor as yourself. There is no other commandment greater than these." Mark 12:31

Jesus continued His answer to the scribes with an additional commandment that was an extension of the first. Notice that "commandment" in this verse is singular—these two commandments are essentially one commandment. In this verse, I see two ways to look at how we can love our neighbor as we love ourselves. First consider that many people love themselves in a selfish kind of way. They want things to be the way they want, when they want, how they want. So on one hand it may appear that we *can* love our neighbor because we love ourselves. But what will that love look like?

On the other hand, there are many people who do not love themselves but instead reject themselves. In that case it would seem very difficult to love one's neighbor. What will that love look like?

Both scenarios give us different pictures of distorted love that cause us to love our neighbor *the same way we love ourselves.* Therefore, it seems imperative that we learn to love ourselves properly first, before we try to love our neighbor. Loving ourselves properly has been spoken to at length in our Grace and Union chapter.

Application: If you still struggle with loving yourself properly, take time to go back through the chapter on Grace and Union. Talk to a trusted friend who knows grace and healing. God wants you to know how loved and accepted you are by Him, not only for your own benefit, but so that you may experience love and intimacy with Jesus that allows true love to flow back and forth with others.

"Be devoted to one another in brotherly love. . ." Romans 12:10.

"Greater love has no one than this that one lay down his life for his friends." John 15:13

In these two verses we have instructions about how we can love others with brotherly, friendship love. Webster defines the word "devoted" as, "dedicated; very loving; loyal, faithful." Unfortunately in many families and communities, the dogs exhibit more devotion to people than other people do. Brothers are estranged from brothers and have even fought wars against each other. Jesus calls us to love one another with His authentic love.

Hopefully you have a person who is devoted to you and who has your best interest at heart. If so, look at that relationship with a grateful heart and seek intimacy with Jesus along the same lines. If not, ask God to bring you such a person while you keep learning to know Jesus better. Those with whom we love and bond shape our choices and our identities more than just trying to think right thoughts and make right choices.[73]

As we read in the second verse, Jesus has shown us how to love. He loves us beyond measure, more than any earthly love we have, and He has proven it by laying down His life. This is how He loves you, even if such love is hard for you to imagine.

In an extreme case we might be called to lay down our life for someone we love, but more often, "laying down our lives for a friend" means being called to unselfishness. Good parents do this continuously. When we take time out of our busy schedules to make dinner for a sick friend or call a friend to get together for coffee, we have given up some of

---

[73] Wilder, *Joy Starts Here*, page 215

our valuable time for someone else. When there has been conflict with someone, we lay down our life via giving up our pride to talk with them and try to work it out.

Time, attention, humility and material possessions are valued costs we pay for being unselfish. What we want to do, or learn how to do, is to be able to lay down our lives for those we love with the same kind of joy as Jesus did when He *literally* laid down His life. I will not soon forget the sacrifice that my son, Greg and his wife, Chris, made for me to live with them for ten years. They gave me a place to live, paid my health insurance, gave me freedom to enjoy life without working full time and loved me unconditionally. My son, Bob and his wife, Amy, helped me buy an air conditioner when I lived by myself and didn't have one. They bought me a laptop. My daughter, Jodi and her husband, Rick, pay me generously for keeping their boys while Jodi works part-time. My son, Jim and his wife, Elizabeth, fill me with joy when I visit them and their family and I have an open invitation to live there should I need to move again. Although not physical, these for whom I once "laid down my life," now love me in a similar way.

> *Application:* Is there a place that Jesus is prompting you to "lay down your life" for someone? Do you have a friend or family member who needs your time or attention? Is there anyone who needs your forgiveness or whom you need to forgive? If so, purpose to take necessary steps to show your love to them this week.

". . . fixing our eyes on Jesus, the author and finisher of our faith, who for the joy set before Him, endured the cross. . ." Hebrews 12: 2

We have been looking at various aspects of love—God's love for us, ours for each other, and love for ourselves. The greatest love was the love of Jesus on the Cross. Quite often we think about the pain and suffering that Jesus endured, but we don't often remember that joy was part of the picture. How could Jesus "endure with joy?" How do love and joy go together? What does that mean for us today?

The first picture that comes to my mind of how I have "endured for the joy set before me" is a common one—having a baby. All of us who have birthed a baby know the pain involved during labor and the joy upon hearing that first cry and seeing that little red face. Perhaps others can identify with the pain of practicing and working out before a big game, or with all the hours needed to practice an instrument before a performance. Emotionally, most of us can identify with those times that we have found it difficult to push through in a relationship because of conflict, but we "endured" because we wanted to work things out and be together. The joy set before Jesus was that He knew He would be restored to the Father, but also that we would be restored to Them—intimacy would be possible. Love and joy go together, especially when we need to push through a tough spot.

Dr. Wilder defines joy as, "Someone is glad to be with me. I am the sparkle in someone's eyes." A love that "endures for the joy set before it" is something all of us desire—we long for connection both earthly and heavenly. That desire for intimacy with others and with Jesus drives us to persevere when the going gets rough, and that joy set before us is what fuels the drive.

There are times in our lives when it's very hard to push through a rough spot. If we're struggling to push through, it might be a sign that we need to take care of ourselves. We might need to lower stress and build joy by relaxing with people who are glad to be with us and/or doing something fun. Remember the devotion on loving our neighbors as we love ourselves—Mark 12:31? Taking care of ourselves by building joy gives us more capacity to love well when times are hard. Stress is much easier to handle when our joy is full.

Regardless of what is going on around us, Jesus is always glad to be with us and always loves us. Whatever we need or whatever He calls us to do, He will be there for us. He created us for joy and bonding with others.

> *Application:* Can you think of a time that you have endured so that you could be close to someone else? Is there a place that you need to take care of yourself, build some joy and regroup in order to love better and push through? Do you really know that you are the "sparkle in Jesus' eyes? Think on that and push through whatever it takes to find the intimacy you long for.

"In Thy presence is fullness of joy." Psalm 16:11

". . . for He Himself has said, 'I will never desert you nor will I ever forsake you.'" Hebrews 13:5b

We looked at how enduring for future joy can bring us through rough spots, now we see that present joy sustains us daily. In the chapter on Faith, devotion James 1: 1-2, we saw that joy would bring us through difficult circumstances as we stay in close communication with Jesus. Here the Psalmist confirms that "fullness of joy" happens when we experience the Lord's presence. Remember our definition of joy—someone is glad to be with me? Remember the longing we all have for intimacy, validation and comfort? Jesus is the answer for those longings—He is always glad to be with us regardless of the circumstances. That means we are never alone and can always be "in joy" with Him. He is always present whether we realize it or not. His very name, Immanuel, means "God with us." (Matthew 1:23)

I'm reminded of my friends, Scott and Debbie, whose family went through a tornado when their children were small. Rain poured, thunder crashed and lightening filled the sky. The children whimpered with fear as the storm raged around their house. Though they were scared, too, Scott and Debbie remained calm as the family headed for the basement. Soon they realized they were going to have to hide in the crawl space under their house. All over the neighborhood, trees were uprooting and falling over. While the family huddled under the house on the dirt floor among the cobwebs, they heard a tree fall on their roof. But in spite of the scary storm, everyone was glad to be together. The family experienced "joy" as Scott and Debbie each held a child on their lap, prayed, sang songs and comforted the children until the storm ended. In the same way, Jesus' intimate presence is where we find joy in our storms. We can "sit in His lap" and trust His word that He is always with us.

> **Application:** Throughout life you will experience storms. You can go through them believing that you are all alone, forsaken and hopeless—or you can go through your storms hearing Jesus' reassurances that He is there and in control. If you are in a storm now, ask Him to show you where He is in that storm. Be still and listen for His reply.

"For who is our hope of joy or crown of exultation? Is it not even you, in the presence of our Lord Jesus at His coming? For you are our glory and joy." 1Thessalonians 2:20

Here we see another aspect of how love and joy go together. Paul is rejoicing with the people of Thessalonica with whom he has developed a close relationship, led to Christ, and mentored. They've become part of Paul's legacy. They are connected. After leaving their city under duress from angry Jewish leaders, Paul wonders how the people are doing. He writes back and discovers they are doing well. Nothing gives a leader more joy than to see his people learning, growing, and maturing. Nothing brings more joy to parents' hearts than to see their children be loving, kind, mature, and in healthy bonded relationships with others.

Webster tells us that bonding is "the development of close relationships between family members or friends." Learning, growing, maturing and being close with others all happen best within strong love bonds. Dr. Wilder gave me some insights that helped me understand "love bonds" and why they are essential to strong and healthy connections with others. Here are some characteristics of a love bond: 1) A strong love bond allows negative and positive feelings to be expressed but does not want the bond to be broken. 2) Love allows the other person to feel their feelings without fear of being rejected. 3) Love bonds do not get broken regardless of how intense things get. (This does not apply to abuse.) 4) When we have a close connection with someone, there will be friction that shows us things in *our* hearts that we need to allow God to work on and heal so that our relationships will be better.[74]

As we can see from these statements, it's within the context of relationships that are characterized by strong love bonds that people find stability. In a relationship that has a strong love bond, it's okay to make mistakes or have a bad day. We don't have to fear that we will be abandoned even if our quirks and annoyances get exposed. Parents, leaders, bosses, and others who are people-helpers will be more effective in helping others when they develop relationships based on healthy, love bonds.

Love bonds make it possible for us to connect closely with others and enjoy their presence. In these loving relationships, we get an earthly experience of what Jesus wants with us—intimacy with Him. Just as we want to connect with others, He loves having that close relationship with us. Like us, Jesus loves watching His children enjoy closeness with each other.

---

[74] E. James Wilder, Ph.D., *The Red Dragon Cast Down*, Page 321

> ***Application:*** Do you have at least one strong, love bond? Do you have a relationship where you know that you will be loved regardless of your quirks and wounded places? Are you experiencing the intimate love bond that Jesus offers to you? Talk to Him with an open heart about your needs and wants—listen for His assurances.

"Iron sharpens iron, so one man sharpens another." Proverbs 27:17

When we are growing a love bond with someone, their love for us will bring up things we need to look at in ourselves, and vice versa. We need to see this as a good thing and not run away from building a love bond for fear of seeing a place we need to grow or some pain we need to work through. God does the same thing with us. When we get close to Him, we will see places we need to grow. But He does not condemn or punish us for these rough places; He shows us gently. Likewise, in our love bonds with one another, we want to work out kindly what gets brought out in each other. All of us have hidden attitudes and motives that we're not aware of until a close loved one helps us see them—or aggravation brings them up.

When, after living more or less alone for ten years, I moved in with my friend, Margie, God showed me that I had become accustomed to being non-relational at times, mostly because I could do whatever I wanted to do and didn't have to talk very much. Now I had someone come in from work each night who wanted to talk and I needed to be ready to interact and hear about her day and share life with her.

If we're willing, God uses the people to whom we are close to teach us much about love. Because it's inevitable that we will get annoyed by a friend's or loved one's quirks, we will have many opportunities to practice loving others unconditionally. Loving others in spite of their quirks is proof of a love bond because we allow each other both positive and negative emotions without breaking the bond. Sharing life in love bonds means the bonds work any time, and we are willing to grow where needed. Everyone benefits as they work through problems and return to joy.

When there are love bonds, it's easy to say to those who need God, "We're part of a family that never ends, and we want God to use what we have with Him and others to bring you into that family."[75] Everyone needs unconditional love and giving it changes both the giver and the receiver.

Application: Do you know when you are being non-relational, when you don't want to be bothered or share life at that moment? Begin to notice when you don't want to be with someone you usually like to be with. Do the "tapping exercise" from devotion Colossians 3:15 in the chapter on Rest and Peace to get your relational circuits back on.[76] Notice which quirks *you* have that might be annoying to those around you. Allow God to bring you through to new places of love. Purpose to overlook at least one quirk from another person you love.

<hr>

[75] From a conversation with Dr. Wilder

[76] Exercise taken from *Belonging Facilitator Workbook*, Ed Khouri, E. James Wilder, Shepherd's House Inc. P.O. Box 40096, Pasadena, CA 91114 page 59; www.thrivingrecovery.org

"The thief comes only to steal, and kill and destroy; I came that they might have life and might have it abundantly."John 10: 10

"For this reason the Father loves Me, because I lay down My life that I may take it again. No one has taken it away from Me, but I lay it down on my own initiative." John 10:18

Love bonds are not the only kind of bonds we make as relational beings—we also make fear bonds. In the first verse here, we can see clearly the difference between love bonds and fear bonds; the contrast between Satan's mission and Jesus' mission. One comes to destroy; the other comes to give abundant life. Love brings life; fear brings destruction.

Fear bonds come from wanting to be close to someone of whom we are afraid. Many people experience fear bonds while growing up. If as a child, we didn't have a choice but to be in a bond with someone we feared, that marks us with a bent towards fear bonds instead of love bonds. Designed by God for joy-filled relationships, we can want connection so badly we may choose to stay in a fear bond with someone who does not truly love us, or even worse, someone who abuses us. Growing up in fear bonds can affect our view of God so that we form a fear bond with Him. Fear bonds need to be healed and replaced with love bonds so that we can experience loving intimacy with Jesus and others. When faced and healed, fear bonds die and fall away. Unlike fear, as we see in our second verse, love bonds survive death.

Jesus' love for us survived the Cross. We easily see the love He had for the thief that repented, the love He had for Mary as He gave her to John's care, and how He said to God, "Father, into Thy hands I commit My spirit." (Luke 23:46) Even though the Father sent Jesus to die, the love between them was not affected by His death. We know for ourselves how we continue to love those we have lost even when we can't be with them. The opposite is true of fear. Fear *is* affected by death.

When a fear comes true, it turns to dust and blows away. The fear no longer holds us captive. I know this is true because I've experienced it. I feared failure and rejection. The result of going through a divorce was that I faced and experienced rejection and failure on many levels. It was painful to go through, but I lived and grew and found intimacy with Jesus. I don't fear failure anymore and most of the time I don't fear rejection. I know what to do when I experience pain, failure and rejection because those fears came true and turned to ashes. Through facing my fears and getting healing, I've learned that I don't want to live in fear. I don't want others to live that way either. I've seen life come out of "the death of fear."[77]

Application: Is there a place in your life that the "thief" is trying to destroy you because of fear? Consider getting with someone who can help you face the fear and go through it so that it will turn to dust and blow away. Talk to Jesus who loves you more than you can know—tell Him about the fears and draw on His love to set you free. Fears have less power when exposed.

"Weeping may last for the night, but a shout of joy comes in the morning." Psalm 30:5b

"Do not be grieved, for the joy of the LORD is your strength." Nehemiah 8:10

It might seem odd that I would choose two verses about grief to look at in a chapter about love, joy and bonding. I have learned a powerful truth: the "joy of the Lord" provides us with the strength to face times of grief.

Something else I know: we cannot have strong love bonds with others without encountering grief along the way. We all know someone who has grown bitter with loss. Or someone who lost hope when something in their life ended. It's hard to experience intimacy with God or others when bitterness and feelings of hopelessness overwhelm us.

---

[77] Information on fear and love from conversations with Dr. Wilder

The Psalmist and Nehemiah remind us that grief is part of life. In II Samuel 12, David mourned the loss of His first child. Jesus wept over Jerusalem; He grieved with Mary and Martha when their brother, Lazarus, died. (John 11:35; Luke 19: 41) All of us will experience grief at some time or another throughout life. We may question what to do with such pain. How can joy be part of it? Nehemiah gives us the solution—in our grief, we keep choosing to "cry out to the Lord" as David did, instead of getting stuck internalizing the feelings that come with loss.[78] We talk to Jesus; we seek His guidance and His presence. We trust that He is always glad to be with us. "The joy of the Lord is our strength" to get through grief and maintain intimacy with Jesus.

> ***Application:*** When you experience grief, let yourself feel what you need to feel while talking to Jesus and trusting that He is feeling your grief with you. He wants you to know how glad He is to be with you every moment so that His joy will be your strength and, in time, your grief will turn to joy because of His presence.

"But I say to you, love your enemies, and pray for those who persecute you." Matthew 5:44

This is a difficult verse to comprehend and live out. The words do not distinguish between people who are hard to get along with and people who might be abusing us. It's an important distinction. In an abusive situation, we need help from others in order to find safety. For our consideration here, I want to look at "enemies" as those people who are

---

[78] Psalm 130:1 "Out of the depths I have cried to Thee, O LORD." Also, Psalms 30:2, 8; 77: 1-2; 119:145; 120:1

hard to get along with and/or those who do not like us rather than those who might be abusive.

Sometimes we have people in our lives who make us feel "persecuted" because they have difficult personalities, they love to be disagreeable or they just love to argue. We cannot always get away from them. They are not easy to love.

Jesus says He can love these people through us as easily as those who are easy to love, even if it doesn't come naturally to us. He loved us when we were His enemies. This is upside down from what modern culture teaches us. Modern culture advocates retaliation or rejection when there are disagreements or differences. When we have a relationship that is difficult and disagreeable, our response can follow the culture's with retaliation or rejection, or it can go another way—we ask Jesus to love them through us. Sometimes a person may be won over by our love when we don't retaliate but keep on loving them where they are.

Love is very powerful when it's willing to bear another's difficult personality. The power comes from being willing to hurt when it is not deserved. Just as Jesus suffered on the Cross when He did not deserve the pain, if we love an "enemy" we become the source of something good and love flows through us.[79] Loving our enemies sends a very strong message that is difficult to ignore.

When we first love a difficult person, our love may bring more negative out of them because they don't know what to do with God's kind of love. They may act worse towards us. As we persevere, there is hope we may win them over. We are basing this kind of powerful love on our identity in Christ—the only way to pull it off. God operates from the certainty that if we know Him, we will love Him. Satan does not care about love—he traffics in fear so people will not find God. He wants us to focus on how difficult this person is and react to them in fear or anger. He knows if we fear the pain of loving an "enemy" we will back down and he will win.[80]

---

[79] Thoughts from conversations with Dr. Wilder.

[80] Ideas in this chapter from Dr. Wilder are either from *Red Dragon Cast Down* as noted or from personal phone conversations.

In order to love a difficult person we have to break through a couple of fears. First we have to be willing to let Jesus love the difficult person through us—we have to accept that we have an "enemy." Secondly, we have to be willing to love someone who may not return the love. Loving through Christ's power without fear will thwart Satan's mission. He wants to keep us from loving our enemies and he wants to keep the other person from finding God's love. It's a mature but worthy calling to let Jesus love a difficult person through us. It will draw us into more intimacy with Him because we will have to be in constant contact with Him as we pray for our "enemy" and for ourselves to be a place from which His love flows out.

> ***Application:*** Do you have someone in your life who is very difficult to love and feels like an "enemy?" Is there a way you can show them love in spite of your fear of how they will respond? Do you pray for them? Don't give up.

"Above all keep fervent in your love for one another, because love covers a multitude of sins." I Peter 4: 8

As we love others around us, in some cases we can over look offenses and mistakes. The Greek word here for "sins" means "miss the mark." I like to think that one way for our love to cover a multitude of sins is that we not be perfectionists. Let's overlook each others' quirks and annoying habits; let's pick our battles. Do you suppose that Jesus does that for us? Of course He does! And He will teach us how to let Him do it in and through us if we allow Him to do so. Choosing not to be a perfectionist brings lots of intimacy because when we are not focused on behavior, we can see other people's hearts. When I feel annoyed by a friend, I turn my thoughts to how grateful I am for the generosity and encouragement he/she brings to our friendship. I remember how much he/she loves me. I ask

Jesus to keep me from nagging or picking at him/her over things that are just "vanilla," not really wrong.

Aren't you glad that Jesus does not condemn us for every little thing we do wrong and loves us just as we are? He sees the areas in which He wants us to grow, but loves us while we are growing.

> *Application:* Is there someone in your life who annoys you? What positives can you focus on about that person that will help you see their heart? Are you a perfectionist? If so, let Jesus teach you how to look past quirks and annoyances to your own and other people's hearts. Let Him teach you that it's okay for you, and others, to mess up.

"Beloved, let us love one another, for love is from God and everyone who loves is born of God and knows God. The one who does not love does not know God for God is love" 1 John 4: 7-8

This verse teaches us a wonderful truth—"God is love." God does not *have* love or just *do* love, He *is* love; love is His essence; love is all that He is and all that can come forth from Him. This is a huge concept, often misunderstood. All over the world people mistakenly see God as uncaring, wrathful, a punisher; someone to fear. It's common for people to mistake their own consequences as punishment, and think God is angry. Such views of God are evidence that many do not really know Him and are projecting human attributes onto Him. God cannot do anything but love.

As humans, our perspective on situations is so limited. We get tangled up in questions such as, "Why does a good God let bad things happen?" We focus on our "whys" and argue over how God fits into the situations of life instead of realizing that He is love and knows what is best far beyond what we can see or know. It seems easier to argue and/or refuse to give in to God than to cry out to Him for comfort and trust Him.

I learned to take God at His word—that He is love—as various difficulties came into my life. Three of my children had major illnesses when they were small—one with a heart condition, two with seizures. I had to trust God for food, milk, bills and income while in the ministry. I went through a divorce. I went through a very painful move from the place I called home. During any of these painful events it would have been easy to believe God is not love because the circumstances, and sometimes the relationships, felt painful at the time, but with each I chose to believe that He knows best and can do nothing that is not love. I have never found God lacking in comfort or provision. He has never let me down; He has never left me.

If you can get hold of how truly loving God is, intimacy will flourish because you will see that He is all-powerful, all-loving and in control of all that comes into your life—He cares more than you can even imagine. (We will look at this concept further in the next chapter.) When we are born of God and know His love, we are able to love others with that kind of love.

Application: There is nothing you can do to make God love you more; there is nothing you can do to make God love you less. There is no good deed that can get God to love you more than He already does; there is no sin that you can do that will keep, or stop, God from loving you. Hold on to that when you are not sure about circumstances in your life! He knows best.

"And may you have the power to understand, as all God's people should, how wide, how long, how high, and how deep his love is." Ephesians 3:18 *New Living Translation*

"But God demonstrates His own love toward us, in that while we were yet sinners, Christ died for us." Romans 5:8

"These things have I spoken unto you. . . that your joy may be made full." John 15:11

Truly comprehending the depths of God's love for us is almost like chasing the wind—it is something we cannot see but we do experience.

Just as there are times when the wind can be so powerful we are in awe of what it can do, and other times it whispers softly on our cheeks and slightly lifts our hair, encounters with God can send us to our knees or simply warm our hearts. Sometimes we feel His presence and love, other times we know it by faith.

Experiencing God's love changes us just as the winds shift the sand in a desert. His love uncovers our fears and hurts and then heals them. His love changes how we feel about ourselves and our failures. We will never be the same after experiencing it first-hand because all of us long to be loved and delighted in and have a place to belong. Knowing His love makes it easier to overlook others' annoyances and love them unconditionally—even those who do not love us back. The love of Christ brings intimacy and makes our joy full.

Application: Have you truly experienced God's love and care for you or are there still places that you doubt? Talk to someone who can help you "shift the sand" in your life and uncover anything that is blocking you from experiencing His love. He loves you because you are you and nothing you have done can keep Him away. Seek His fullness of joy until you find it.

FEELINGS AND APPEARANCES: BARRIERS TO INTIMACY

"While we look not at the things which are seen, but at the things which are not seen; for the things which are seen are temporal, but the things which are not seen are eternal." II Corinthians 4:18

How we handle emotions and how circumstances appear to us greatly affect the intimacy we have with Jesus. In this verse, Paul teaches us how to handle our feelings and circumstances in a way that builds strong, healthy relationships. Paul tells us to "look not at the things which are seen," but instead to focus on "the things which are not seen." The perspective from which we are looking at our circumstances is vitally important because we will interpret the reality of our circumstances depending on how we look at them.

Our friend Dan Stone called these two views of our current circumstances: "above the line" or "below the line." Let's look at a chart that will show us some other synonyms we can use to describe each realm:

Eternal (above); invisible; changeless; timeless; ultimate reality; complete, finished and whole

---

Temporal (below); visible; temporary; natural; created; appearances; beginning and end; time

As we can see, things above the line are attributes of God and often have to be believed by faith. They are *not* tangible. Below the line characteristics are easier to observe and can make us believe that they are more true than what God says because they *are* tangible. Conquering this struggle to believe the eternal and invisible as ultimate reality over what we can see and touch will increase the trust and intimacy we have with Jesus.

Here are three ways that living "above the line" will increase intimacy. First, God designed the world to work by faith as we looked at in the Faith chapter. When you look at the diagram, you can see that Jesus lived His life "above the line" doing what He saw the Father do.[81] As Jesus lived His life, the Father's heart became visible as Jesus healed people and raised the dead; as He fed multitudes and He walked with his men. Jesus wants to live through us today, continuing to do through us what He sees the Father doing.

Second, when we distinguish the two realms it helps us understand our true identity in Christ as we looked at in the Grace and Union chapter. It helps us separate who we are from what we do, freeing us to live and walk in Christ. When we see our circumstances from above the line, it helps keep them in perspective and they are less overwhelming. Living above the line makes relationships better because we see others the way God sees them.

Third, living above the line brings more fulfillment in life because God designed us to get our satisfaction from Him. There is no pleasure or person below the line that will truly satisfy. There is nothing below the line that equals true life that can only be found in God and His Son.[82]

When we look at circumstances in our lives from "above the line," God's truth may not feel or look true in the moment, but I've found God to be faithful when I choose to believe what is "above the line'" over what is visible "below the line." In 1984 while our family was living financially dependent on God for any income, three of us spent time in the hospital that year for one reason or another. I wondered if we should stop doing ministry and find a job with a paycheck. After discussing the possibility of looking for a job, we decided to hold on to this verse in II Corinthians because we wanted to get our satisfaction from God. In a few short

---

[81] John 5:19

[82] Line illustration from Dan Stone, *The Rest of the Gospel*, pages 28-31

months, God provided all the money needed to pay off the hospital bills—and confirmed we were to continue to minister and trust Him for our income. [83]

> ***Application:*** What circumstances are you facing that pull at you to decide that "reality" is what you can see and touch? Can you draw a line in the air and tell Jesus you want to live "above the line" and trust Him? Make that choice and talk to Him about your needs. Let Him reassure you that He is with you, that you are valuable and loved, and that He alone brings you satisfaction.

"For the word of God is living and active and sharper than any two-edged sword, and piercing as far as the division of soul and spirit, of both joint and marrow and able to judge the thoughts and intentions of the heart." Hebrews 4:12

As we learn "the division between soul and spirit," we will be less likely to let feelings and circumstances keep us from intimacy with Christ. We looked briefly at the soul and spirit in the devotion on I Thessalonians 5: 23 in the Grace and Union chapter; here we will look at the differences a little closer.

Have you ever felt a temptation to do something dishonest such as keep extra change that a cashier mistakenly gave you? You feel like you want to keep it, but something else feels like you better not. These two feelings are the differences between the soul and spirit. The writer of Hebrews tells us that the word of God is alive, will pierce our

---

[83]To see more about how choosing to live "above the line" looked for our family, see the book *Jesus Never Fails, Stories of God's Faithfulness,* www.lulu.com/barbaramoon, 2010; Story from page 72

understanding of the soul and spirit, and divide the two, showing us by which one we are living. Hebrews gives us two analogies that make it clearer—"joints and marrow" and "thoughts and intentions of the heart." I like how Dan Stone explains the two analogies:

> The Holy Spirit didn't speak to me through the division of soul and spirit because I didn't understand that. He didn't speak to me through the joints and marrow phrase because I'm not a doctor. Finally I got it by the phrase about thoughts and intentions of the heart. My thoughts and feelings can be going one direction and what I know in my spirit can be experiencing something different.
>
> As a believer, I know the intent of my heart. It is fixed. Pushed to the wall, I want to please God. But I can have thoughts and feelings that differ from the intent of my heart. For the first time in my awareness I experienced the reality of spirit.[84]

Laurie Hills, a friend of mine and Dan's also spoke often about this verse in Hebrews. As an artist, when Laurie looks at this verse, she sees it as a heart with a sword dividing the heart through the middle:[85]

---

[84] *The Rest of the Gospel*, page 67 paraphrased

[85] Laurie's heart diagram taken from *Jewels For My Journey*, by Barbara Moon, pages 26-32 www.amazon.com and www.lulu.com/barbaramoon, used with Laurie's permission.

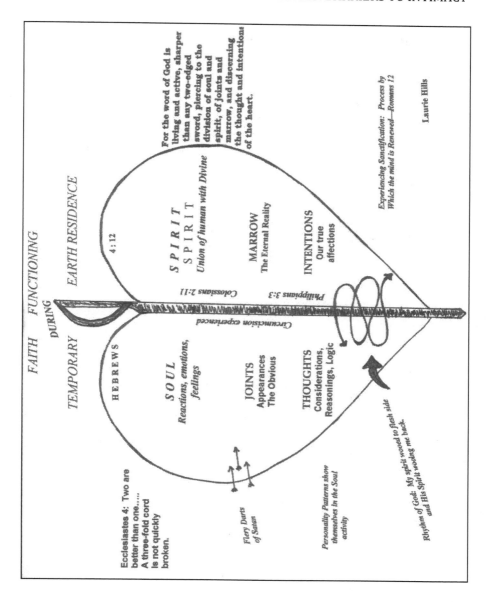

On the soul side are the soul's characteristics: Emotions, Reactions, Appearances and Thoughts. These are un-dependable and fleeting; not the things upon which to base our lives. The spirit side of Laurie's heart drawing has one characteristic—Union of human with Divine.

Now, using Laurie's heart diagram let's look at where the words of Hebrews 4:12 fit with dividing soul and spirit. "Joints" go on the soul side, "marrow" on the spirit. "Thoughts" go on the soul side, "intentions" on the spirit side. Laurie explains the joints and marrow by picturing an elbow. The "joint" is seen when the elbow bends, but the "marrow" is inside, invisible, and where the life is. "Joints" are appearances and emotions; "marrow" is God Himself dwelling and working in us. We see the appearances and feelings first when something negative happens. This shakes us up, and disturbs our inner peace, but that confusion is a sign for us to turn toward the "marrow," God in us.

When we are a believer, the "intention of our heart" since salvation has been to please God and love Him with all our heart. Our thoughts and feelings can take us many places, even into sin, that are not pleasing to God, but when we turn to the "intentions of our heart" by faith, we find intimacy with Christ and experience His presence.

> *Application:* Can you think of a place where you are confusing the soul and spirit by believing your feelings and appearances are what should rule your life? Ask Jesus to pierce your understanding between the soul and spirit and show you the intentions of your heart—that you truly want to love, obey and serve Him—so that you might live in more intimacy with Him.

"Be angry and yet do not sin; do not let the sun go down on your anger." Ephesians 4:26

As we look at different ways that emotions and feelings can be barriers to intimacy, let's look at an emotion that commonly bothers most of us. Paul tells us here that we can be angry and not sin. Most of the people I have talked to through the years believe that any anger is a sin and thus avoid anger. If we think anger and other negative emotions are wrong, we will suppress the feelings. Suppressing feeling is not healthy. Feelings in and of themselves are "just feelings" and can be expressed in healthy ways. On the other hand, feelings can be expressed in ways that hurt others. Let's look at these two ideas separately.

Dan Stone gives us a visual picture of how to look at our feelings as "just feelings" by picturing children on a swing. Dan compares the swing to the three parts of a person that we have looked at—our human spirit, our soul and our body.[86]

When children jump into a swing they do not pay any attention to the place the swing is attached. They just swing. The human spirit is the place where our emotional swing is attached. The spirit

---

[86] We looked at these in the Grace and Union chapter, devotion I Thessalonians 5:23.

is fixed; it does not fluctuate. It's in union with the Holy Spirit, secure and safe. (John 15:4; Psalm 19:14; I Corinthians 6:17) God is our Anchor—dependable and unchanging. (Hebrews 6: 17-19)

On the other hand, the swing seat, which represents our personality (our soul) and our body, is changeable. Our thoughts and emotions swing all the time, changing moment by moment, going all over the place at times. Our feelings are meant to swing. But we don't like the swing to swing. We think it's more spiritual if the swing doesn't swing; therefore, we try to nail it up on the side that we think is spiritual—so we can have only "good" feelings.

Here we are again, by rejecting our changing emotions, trying to figure out what is good and bad—trying to figure out what are good thoughts, good feelings and good behavior. But just thinking good thoughts, feeling good feelings and doing good things do not get us to God or make us spiritual. We are eating from the wrong tree again; trying to get life by our own efforts. Only God can give life. Eve thought it would be good to eat the fruit of the tree of the knowledge of good and evil, but it was not God telling her to eat it. (Genesis 3:6)

We are never going to get the swing, our thoughts and feelings, to stop—because God made them to swing—He made us as thinking and feeling beings. Our thoughts and feelings change all the time. It's easy to feel as if we are "like the surf of the sea driven and tossed by the wind." (James 1:6)

Why did God make our emotions to swing? Because swinging emotions are the best way to get us to live by faith, to live out of who we are and who He is instead of by appearances and feelings. God uses the operation of the swing (thoughts and feelings) to push us into living out of the spirit. He wants us to stop trying to "crucify self," by taking hold of our thoughts and feelings and trying to nail them all on the "good" side. That only leads to us failing and going back under guilt when it doesn't work. We are going to try to stop the swing until we see that God means it to swing so that we will exercise faith.[87]

Knowing that feelings are meant to swing does not mean that we ignore them or just go about letting them out indiscriminately. Feeling angry is just a feeling until we use it to hurt someone. Learning what to do with anger and other negative emotions is part of good parenting and child development. When we're angry or someone is angry with us, we need to know how to talk out our differences in a calm manner and return to joy and be glad to be reconnected in the relationship.[88] Forgiveness might be necessary. If we did not have an opportunity to learn these important skills, we will likely not have the ability to healthily handle our anger, and either we will stuff the anger, blow up on others, or ignore the effects our anger has on people around us. What we *do* with anger determines if it is "just a feeling" or if it is sin.

Anger can be a signal that something needs to be discussed, something is hurting us that needs to be addressed, or there is something we need to forgive or let go of. There may be an underlying reason for our anger that is amplifying it and making it stronger than the immediate situation in which the anger is occurring. When we feel anger that is out of proportion to a situation, it's a signal that something from our *past* needs to be healed by Jesus. When anger is "just a feeling" and not amplified by underlying, unresolved reasons, we will find it easier to "not sin."

Application: Do you struggle with anger that you stuff or that you express in hurtful ways? Does it feel like you don't know how to handle anger? Jesus wants to know about your anger and is ready to listen. He wants to heal unresolved anger from your past. Talk to a trusted friend who can remain okay with you while you feel angry and help you find healing as you learn how to handle your anger.

---

[87] *The Rest of the Gospel*, pages 69-72 paraphrased. Also see Hebrews 11:6a, II Corinthians 4:18 and 5: 7

[88] For more information on learning skills for returning to joy from negative emotions, go to www.lifemodel.org or www.thrivetoday.org

". . . and He said to them, 'Let us go over to the other side of the lake.' And they launched out. But as they were sailing along He fell asleep, and a fierce gale of wind descended upon the lake they began to be swamped and to be in danger. And they came to Him and woke Him up, saying, 'Master, Master we are perishing!' And being aroused, He rebuked the wind and the surging waves, and they stopped, and it became calm." Luke 8: 22-24

Let's look at another emotion that is commonly a barrier to intimacy— fear. There have been many songs written and pictures painted about this famous passage in Luke where Jesus sleeps through a dangerous storm. Fear overwhelms the disciples as they hear the fierce wind and see the huge waves that threaten to swamp their fishing boat. Most of us can identify with their fear when we face the storms that come into our lives in the form of financial problems, health issues, rebellious children and loss of loved ones. Fear is often our first reaction.

When my daughter, Jodi, was about thirteen, an accident happened that is probably at the top of my list of fearful events. Our family was camping with friends, Jan and Bill Crossan and their two kids. Bill was pulling Jodi and his daughter, Kelly, behind their boat in a large inner tube. As he circled around near the shore, I could see that the inner tube was going to hit a rocky retaining wall there in front of me on the shore. My heart seemed to stop and my stomach lurched at the thought while fear screamed in my head. Sure enough, the tube hit the wall—but it bounced off and stopped. I jumped into the lake and swam out to the tube. Jodi had a cut on her elbow and the girls were bruised, but otherwise they were not hurt. I was so thankful that God had spared the girls from an extremely bad possibility. As I towed Jodi back to the shore in the tube, my emotions slowly settled as I knew that the girls were safe.

Like the disciples, our first inclination is to feel fear when scary things happen, but to their credit, they knew where to turn. They woke up the Master, probably yelling over the thundering noise of the storm, and watched as Jesus instantly calmed the storm with a word. Fear is a strong emotion that can easily keep us barricaded from intimacy with Jesus. The best way to find peace in our storms is to turn to Him in the fear. Even if He does not change the circumstance in which we find ourselves fearful, His presence will calm us—His children—in the midst of the storm.

Application: Do you have a "storm" thundering around you that is causing you fear? Take note of the disciples' action—they turned to the Master. Tell Him about your "storm" and let Him calm you in the midst. Surround yourself with people who know how to stay calm during "storms."

"And He said to them, 'Where is your faith?' And they were fearful and amazed, saying to one another, 'Who then is this that He commands even the winds and the water and they obey Him?'" Luke 8:25

Jesus calms us in our storms and does not condemn us for our feelings, but in this verse that follows Him calming the storm, we see an important question that Jesus asked the men: "Where is your faith?" I do not think that Jesus was fussing at them; I think He was taking advantage of a teachable moment. Like the disciples, it's easy for us to either overlook or to forget what Jesus has promised, thus allowing fear to be a barrier to intimacy with Him. In the first part of verse 22 in the previous devotion, notice that Jesus had already told the disciples, "Let's go over to the other side." They forgot Jesus' words, they panicked, and they needed reminding: *"You can trust Me, Fellows. I want you to learn that. I am the*

Creator of the storms, and I control them. You do not have to be afraid because I've got it all in my Hands."

While looking for verse addresses in a concordance, I counted twelve times in the Gospels and Acts where Jesus, or angels, said, "Fear not." The most famous place is when the angels appeared to the shepherds to announce the birth of Jesus in Luke 2. In Acts 27:24, an angel told Paul not to be afraid when the ship he was on was sinking. Paul believed God was sending Him to Rome, and he believed the angel who told him no one would perish in the storm. Paul found calm for himself and his shipmates because he held on to God's promise.

I had to trust God in a storm when my second son, Bob, had appendicitis his senior year in high school. His appendix burst right before he was taken to surgery. That night I sat by his bed praying for his safety, clinging to God. I felt scared, but I found some calm in the storm as I talked to God and helped the nurses keep his fever down. Faith is the opposite of fear.

Application: How are you finding calm in your storms? Do you remember God's promises and Jesus' words? Fear not; rely on Jesus' faithfulness and love.

"There is no fear in love; but perfect love casts out fear, because fear involves punishment, and the one who fears is not perfected in love." I John 4:18

Accidents are not the only kind of fears that put up barriers to intimacy with Christ. Emotional fears are strong and prevalent barriers that need to be torn down as well. During my divorce, fear of failure was a close companion. I feared what others would think if we divorced. I feared how I would live if not married. I feared what would happen to our family. I feared failure. I was trying very hard to make things work so none of these fears would come true—I was avoiding the pain of failure. I mistakenly believed that I could do something to avoid the failure, but fighting fears would not make them go away. I was going to have to face them.

Dr. Wilder told me to "Get comfortable with the reality that you will fail. Learn to live with limitations. Limitations and failure are not bad. God knows we are but dust. Don't assume that He has expectations and gets disappointed in us."

I began to get a better hold on the message that trying to avoid failure was fighting a losing battle when Dr. Wilder used an analogy: "No one can talk me into picking up my van. If I really believe I can't, I won't try. If I try—I think I can." The mental picture of trying to pick up my car, something I cannot do, something I cannot control, helped me stop trying to make everything work.

If I would face the fears, Dr. Wilder assured me that when they came true, they would burn to ashes and blow away. They would be gone. I'd never heard anyone say such a thing. Was that possible? In order to face the fears, I had to stop trying to keep them from happening, something I really could not control anyway. I had to feel the pain that went with the fears and hold on to Jesus while He took me through whatever came. Jesus' perfect love would cast out my fears even as the fears came true.

As I faced my fears and they did come true, often beyond my control, I found Dr. Wilder's words to be correct—the fears turned to ashes and blew away. Before the fears came true and blew away, I focused on them, my "emotional knees" shaking. That is a life of worry. After they came true, I did not fear what other people would think; I did not fear failure. I failed and neither God nor the people who mattered deserted me. Love overcame my fear and I grew more intimacy with the Lord.

The picture of me trying to pick up my car has stuck with me over time as I often need to be reminded that there is not much I can control and living in fear does not make anything better. Failure was not the end of the world—and fighting fears is as foolish as trying to pick up a car.

"God has not given us the spirit of fear, but of power and of love and of a sound mind." II Timothy 1:7 KJV

Paul tells us here in II Timothy that overwhelming fear is not of God. There are times that we can turn away from fear to intimacy with God by realizing fear is the opposite of God's love. We have His power to turn from fear because Jesus lives in us. Fear in our minds paralyzes; love and faith free us to hear God. All we have to do is turn to Him and trust Him.

When our first son was in college, about two hours from home, he called one night to tell us he was in the emergency room because he had been hit in the cheek by a thrown softball which had broken his cheek bone. In spite of the fear I felt, I talked with him and told him we would pray for him and see him when he could get home. His dad and I both knew we could not make it to the ER in time to be with him as we would have done if he were home or nearby. Usually a calm person during crises, I was very surprised when, after hanging up the phone, I burst into tears. I had faced many crises that involved ER's and major illnesses, but this was the first time I was not able to be there with one of my children. I did not like that feeling at all. I had to trust Jesus to be there in my place and not fear how my son would get through it. I finished crying, blew my nose and prayed, leaving the fear in Jesus' lap.

"O ye sons of men, how long will ye turn my glory into shame. . .?" Psalm 4:2

Shame is another emotion that frequently keeps us from intimacy with Christ, perhaps one of the most common barriers and often misunderstood. Shame means someone is not pleased with me right now, and the displeasure can be communicated in different ways of correction—one way helps us grow closer to each other; the other makes us feel like we are bad. It seems that the latter is the most common perception of shame, but the former, when understood, will increase our intimacy with Christ and each other. In order to better understand the differences and other similar words used in Scripture, let's look at some definitions from the Greek, the Hebrew and English:

Greek and Hebrew

Shame: disappointment, disgrace, dishonor, ashamed or reproach. These are various words in the Scripture translations.

English—Webster

Shame: the painful feeling of having lost respect of others because of improper behavior.

Disappointment: to fail to satisfy the hopes or expectations of; leave unsatisfied.

Disgrace: being in disfavor because of bad conduct.

Dishonor: loss of honor or respect.

Ashamed: feeling shame because something bad, wrong or foolish was done.

Reproach: accused for a fault to make feel ashamed; rebuke.

Already just from looking at these definitions, it's possible that some of us are feeling tightness in our stomachs. The definitions strongly suggest that something has gone wrong in our behavior and needs correcting. If you were raised in a family where any behavior perceived as "off" was met with what I call "toxic shame," it is likely that thinking about *any* kind of correction sounds demeaning to you. Toxic shame is often verbal, but can be subtly communicated with body language or facial expressions. However the toxic message comes, it says the receiver is bad. Parents who do not separate behavior and personhood often communicate toxic shame when behavior is bad. (See devotion I Peter 3:4 in Grace and Union.)

Adults reared by rejecting discipline or abuse hear "toxic shame messages," whenever someone tries to correct their behavior, even if a toxic shame message is not there. It's very difficult to hear that anything is wrong with me if I don't know that there's another way to look at shame. If toxic shame is all we know, it will be easy to hold God aloof at a distance because we think He feels towards us the way our parents felt—"You are bad because your behavior is bad." According to the Scriptures, feeling ashamed is not supposed to keep us separated from God and others. When handled in love with an understanding of good shame, correction helps us grow and brings us closer together.

Application: Does even talking about shame make your stomach hurt? Jesus wants you to know a different way to look at shame. Good shame messages can bring people closer together. (Ephesians 4:15)

"And hope does not disappoint (*make ashamed, KJV*), because the love of God has been poured out within our hearts through the Holy Spirit who was given to us." Romans 5:5

There is another way to look at shame, especially when we have digested and experienced the truths we looked at in the chapter on Grace and Union. God loves us so much and He has done all that needs to be done for us to have intimacy with Him. He is glad to be with us even when our behavior stinks. He will address the behavior by conviction, but unlike many not-so-good parents, God will not reject us at the same time; He will not say we are bad. The hope we have in Christ will not bring disappointment to God or toxic shame to us. God sees the Holy Spirit in our hearts and separates our behavior from who we are.

Dr. Wilder has greatly influenced my thinking about shame. He defines shame as. "Someone is *not glad* to be with me." Shame is the opposite of joy—"Someone *is* glad to be with me." When our behavior keeps someone from not wanting to be with us, we are not bringing them joy, and if we grew up with toxic shame we will have a misunderstanding of "good shame" if that person tries to speak to our behavior. Through a CD by Dr. Wilder, I came to understand that good shame is when we talk to someone about their behavior *because we want to be close to them*, we want to return to joy and be glad to be together.[89] Good parents understand this when they discipline inappropriate behavior without rejecting their child. Let's look at an example of talking to someone because we want to be close:

> Two sisters grew up with one bullying the other. As adults, the bully continues to show anger when crossed. Other family members are afraid to say anything because the bully may blow up. But what everyone really wants is to be close. A "good shame message" tells the bully that her behavior is making others not want to be with her. If she humbles herself and works on her anger, others will love to be close.

---

[89] *Munchie # 24* can be purchased at www.lifemodel.org or www.thrivetoday.org

Shame (not glad to be together right now) is a legitimate feeling that results from behavior that needs to be addressed. I once heard a speaker say, "That I love you is like a solid line; what I do for you is a dotted line." That statement divides personhood and behavior and helps us see that good shame sends a message about behavior, not about personhood. We can love someone who is not behaving well, but we may not want to be with them until they work on their behavior.

The misunderstandings we have about shame, the lack of separating behavior and personhood and the ways we were reared with toxic shame contribute to a lack of intimacy with Christ and others. As we consider where we have misunderstandings about shame, and as we realize that the purpose for addressing behavior is to be able to be close, hopefully truth will penetrate some of our barriers that make us see God as a wrathful punisher and replace that perspective with closeness. Look at Ephesians 4:15.

> *Application:* Were you reared in a toxic shame environment? Is it difficult for you to give or take correction? Ask Jesus what you need to do or learn in order to be able to be close to those with whom you want to be close when their behavior is not okay. Is shame causing you to hold yourself aloof from God? Consider these truths and have the courage to let down your barriers with God.

"For the Scripture says, 'Whoever believes in Him will not be disappointed.'" (*ashamed, KJV*) Romans 10:11

Let's look now at the word "disappointed," used here in Romans 10, in relation to our discussion about shame. Remember the definition earlier for "disappointing" was "to fail to satisfy the hopes or expectations of; leave unsatisfied." We can easily see that children who are misbehaving are disappointing their parents' hopes and expectations. Correcting disappointing behavior is part of learning right and wrong. Paul tells us here that we who believe in Jesus will never be disappointed or ashamed. Does that mean our Heavenly Father will never correct us in order to teach us right and wrong? Not at all. He will correct us, but He will never give us "toxic shame messages" while He does it. The promise here is that we will not be ashamed or disappointed in Him when we understand who He is and how He looks at us after we receive Jesus. If we don't know Him as He really is, and we misunderstand shame, we will not be able to enjoy intimacy with our Heavenly Father and His Son.

When we don't understand how shame works, we will not only feel that God will disappoint us, we will feel that we are a big disappointment to Him. I remember when I first thought about *not* being a disappointment to God. Most of my life I had believed that I was quite a disappointment to Him because of things I had done or failed to do. One day it dawned on me that Someone who knows everything, even the future, would not be able to be disappointed. How could He be disappointed when He knew what I was going to do before I did it? Yes, He might feel sad, but knowing I was not a disappointment to God made my day. It brought peace to my mind and joy to my heart.

Application: Do you know that you are *not* a disappointment to God? He loves you even when you blow it. Go ahead and take a risk to open up more to Him about whatever is currently bothering you. He already knows all about it, and He wants to be with you no matter what. He will correct you lovingly and without toxic shame.

"For both He who sanctifies and those who are sanctified are all from one Father; for which reason He is not ashamed to call them brethren." Hebrews 2:11

Let's look at another verse that blesses us with God's love through Christ and helps us feel freer to open up to His intimacy. The writer of Hebrews tells us that Christ is not ashamed to call us His brothers and sisters. We who are in Christ, in union with Him, sanctified (made holy) by His blood are truly part of God's family. I'm certain there are many families that are ashamed of others in their family. Siblings and parents are estranged and never speak. Holidays are not joy-filled events. Gossip, hatred, and bitterness permeate relationships with anger, fear and toxic shame. Often, the broken relationships are based on events that could certainly be justified because of someone's behavior and attitude. If we've lived in such an environment, we could easily reason that God has the authority to feel ashamed towards us when we think about actions, attitudes, and sins we have committed. But the writer here is taking us far beyond how we humans treat one another—Jesus, our Sanctifier, is not ashamed of us in any way. We are born of the same Father as He and loved in spite of behavior; we are closer than close—we are one.

One day after my identical twin granddaughters were born, I realized that, for perhaps a few hours or days, they were one person. It was hard to imagine, but interesting to ponder. Thinking about that gave me a glimpse of God's love for us—we Christians are one with Him—He wants to be with us so much that we are one—but we are two. The Father, Son and Holy Spirit are one, but they are three. We are in their family and there is no place in Them for disappointment or disappointing. There is no toxic shame for those who are in Christ Jesus.[90]

Application: Do you have broken relationships because of another's behavior? Talk to Jesus about it and listen to what He might ask you to do. Relationships are about being glad to be together and returning to being glad to be together when disconnects happen. If it's

---

[90] See blogs on *How Shame Shapes Us* at www.barbaramoon.wordpress.com

not an abusive situation, consider talking to the person so that you can restore your closeness. Get a "third party" if necessary. Soak yourself in the truth that you are one with Jesus. (I Corinthians 6:17)

". . . for even Satan disguises himself as an angel of light."II Corinthians 11:14

As we continue to consider how appearances and emotions such as anger, fear and shame can be barriers to intimacy, let's take a look at how Satan comes into the picture. The Gospels tell us he is a liar, a deceiver, the tempter, and an accuser. Paul tells us he often deceives by trying to look like an angel of light. Dr. Bill Gillham proposes that one of the ways Satan tricks and deceives is by speaking to us in first person singular (I, me) using *our own voice* and "old tapes" that fit the lies we believe.[91] Satan was a large part of planting those lies in our minds in the first place. As I considered ways to teach this concept of Satan using first person singular to others, I came up with a chart that helps us see the difference in God's voice and Satan's voice. They are easily distinguishable when we know the difference and recognizing each will help us keep down the barrier caused by guilt over having what we think are bad thoughts or feelings. In order to make it simple, I have called this chart, "Two Voices," realizing that we might have thoughts we call our own. In that case, they would go under whichever list they fit. The chart:

---

[91] *Lifetime Guarantee*, page 103

SATAN'S VOICE:	GOD'S VOICE:
Condemns	Convicts
Performance Based Acceptance	Accepts
Lies	Truth
Loud	Soft (1 Kings 19:11-12)
Selfish	Unconditional love
Discouraging	Encouraging
Worry, Doubts	Trust Me
Fear	Faith and Love
Presses Down	Lifts up
Death Giving	Life Giving
Dark	Light
Sin Conscious	Righteousness Conscious

Certainly there are other points we could come up with, but this list can get us started on recognizing and rejecting lies from the enemy. Anabel Gillham spoke of another way to "analyze the thoughts that invade our thinking processes: We can check to see if, A) This is a condemning thought. B) This thought attacks my character. C) This thought accuses me. D) This thought confuses me. E) This thought is designed to destroy me. F) This thought is not true."

Anabel also recommends adding "In Jesus' name" to any thought to see if it fits with God's voice or the devil's. (The source of this quote is lost as I think I heard it in person.)

Application: Begin today to notice the tone and words to thoughts you have. If the thoughts fit with Satan's voice, hold out your hand like a policeman at an intersection and say, "Stop! That is not God or me." Refuse to take thoughts that condemn you or discourage you. Replace them with God's truth.

". . . And behold the Lord was passing by! And a great and strong wind was rending the mountains and breaking in pieces the rocks before the LORD; but the LORD was not in the earthquake. And after the earthquake, a fire, but the LORD was not in the fire; and after the fire a sound of gentle blowing." I Kings 19: 11-12

We have seen a fairly comprehensive list of ways to determine God's voice from the enemy's voice, one of which was found in this verse in I Kings. Elijah, the Old Testament prophet, had defeated the prophets of Baal and brought down fire upon an altar soaked in water, consuming the wood, the dust, and the stones (18:38). Then he ran away in fear of Queen Jezebel who wanted to kill him. He made a decision based on his feelings in his soul. Elijah was depressed and whining to the Lord about his plight when the Lord told him to stand before Him. God passed by in the form of an earthquake, wind, and fire. God did it; He was in it. But in another sense, God was not in it; the noise was not the deepest understanding Elijah could have of God. Dan Stone says God was telling Elijah, "If you judge reality by what is happening at your soul level, what you see and think and feel, you're going to miss Me."[92]

After the loud earthquake, wind, and fire, Elijah heard something else—a sound of gentle blowing. I love how the King James translates it— "a still small voice." Maybe it was so quiet that Elijah did not hear anything audible. But he knew beyond a shadow of doubt that he was in the presence of God. That's how God talks to us—gently and quietly in our spirits, not in the loudness and emotions of our souls. We will have to listen for what He is telling our spirit even over the loudness and emotions of our souls. And when we know God's voice, we know He has spoken.

---

[92] *The Rest of the Gospel*, page 76

Application: Ask Jesus to show you the difference in the two voices and to teach you to hear His voice. Believe that you are hearing Him when the words fit with His character. Practice listening. Practice believing it is He.

"Although the Lord has given you bread of privation and water of oppression, He, your Teacher will no longer hide Himself, but your eyes will behold your Teacher." Isaiah 30:20

This verse was given as a future prophecy to the Israelites, but it has come true for us because Jesus has come, died, risen, and lives in us. He will teach us His voice.

Years ago I read in an old book about Reece Howells, a British leader and minister who lived during World War II. Mr. Howells was known for his prayer life and his close relationship with God. Someone asked him one day how he knew God's voice. He answered something like this: "You know your mother's voice don't you?"[93] When I read that, immediately I realized that I never had to ask, "Who is this?" when my mother called me on the phone. I always knew her voice. So I asked God, "Teach me to know Your voice as well as I do my mother's." He has been faithful to do that, often by trials and suffering as we looked at in that chapter. I also learned his voice and experienced His faithfulness through having to trust Him financially.

Another way God teaches us to know His voice is by speaking and then waiting to see if we obey. When we obey what we are fairly certain is He, it cements in us that we heard Him. And—it encourages God to keep

---

[93] *Rees Howells Intercessor*, Norman Grubb, Christian Literature Crusade, Fort Washington, PA 19034, 1973

speaking. Sometimes we'll be mistaken, but that's all right with Him, too. I remember when we were raising support to go on staff with Campus Crusade for Christ; I thought God told me if I would fast and pray for a week that He would raise all the support in a month. I didn't know this was very un-realistic—I was new at trusting God for everything—so I fasted. Although the promise did not come true until much later, I did not beat up on myself for mistaking what I thought was God's timing. I went right on loving Him and trusting that He was teaching us all many things through the support-raising time and having to trust Him.

> ***Application:*** As you talk to Jesus this week, notice your thoughts during that time. Notice if you have a "good idea" that might be Him speaking to you. You can run a "test" in your mind to see if you have peace about the idea and if you have what it takes to do the "good idea." If so, obey the thoughts, trusting that it is Jesus. Ask Him to teach you to know His voice as well as you know a dear loved one's voice.

"And as for you, you meant evil against me, but God meant it for good in order to bring about this present result, to preserve many people alive." Genesis 50:20

In our chapter about suffering and trials, we looked at the verses about the "single eye" in the Luke 11:34 devotion and how all things work together for good in the Romans 8:28 devotion. Here in Genesis we see another aspect of how God works out things that might appear to be very negative if we are living below the line, out of our souls, and by appearances. Joseph had been sold into captivity by his jealous brothers. Taken to Egypt, he was imprisoned, falsely accused of rape and left forgotten for years. After God worked to bring Joseph into the Pharaoh's court as an important and powerful official, Joseph had a remarkably successful life. Years later when a famine covered his family's land back in Canaan, his same brothers appeared before him in need of food. This powerful official, unknown to the brothers, could have had all of them executed right on the spot. Instead, he told them who he was, gave them food, and sent them home to bring their people to Egypt to live. Joseph saved his people and was re-united with his father and brothers. He told them, "You meant it for evil, but God meant it for good."

This passage sums up for me, faith, joy in suffering, living above the line and God's loving sovereignty. Practicing this verse changes negatives into positives; practicing this verse turns our hearts to intimacy with God. God might change the negative to a positive without us practicing the truth of the verse, but if we do turn to Him and His intimate love and kindness *during* the difficult circumstance, we will be doubly blessed—we will walk through it with Him and then we will watch Him turn it to some kind of good.

Remember the story about my daughter's boating accident a few pages back in the devotion from Luke 8: 22 where Jesus calmed the storm? Other than the injuries not being too bad, at first glance that fearful accident did not appear to have anything good in it—but I did not tell the whole story in the previous devotion. The rest of Jodi's story fits here with Joseph's comment to his brothers. Jodi had a cut on her elbow, so just to make certain that her elbow wasn't broken, we took her to the emergency room. It only needed stitches. Thanking God for His mercy, I took Jodi home and her dad and Greg went back and packed up the campsite. A few weeks later, as expected, we learned that our insurance covered the ER bill. A few days later, unexpectedly, we learned that Bill's boat insurance also covered the bill. Bill sent us the check from his insurance company, and since the ER bill was paid, we could keep the money. We used that money to get braces for Jodi, a need for which we had been praying and was not visible in our budget. God took something that looked "bad" and used it for good.

Application: Can you think of something in your life that looked bad for a while but God turned to good? Thank Him for that. Are you currently going through something that looks bad? If so, talk to God about it in faith that He will work it out for good in His time. Trust Him no matter the outcome.

"All discipline for the moment seems not to be joyful, but sorrowful; yet to those who have been trained by it, afterwards it yields the peaceful fruit of righteousness." Hebrews 12:11

Discipline is another aspect of our journey that can feel and look "bad." I would like to take a quick look at it in two ways—discipline that we receive from God when our behavior needs tweaking—and self-discipline that we practice in order to grow. Let's begin with God's discipline.

In more than one place we have looked at the truth that, when our behavior needs addressing, God convicts us but He does not condemn us. We saw those differences on our chart of how to distinguish His voice from the enemy's. When God disciplines us for something we have done that He wants to change, we usually have negative feelings about how it feels. Consequences seldom ever feel good at all. We feel sorrowful. But I like this verse here in Hebrews that gives us hope for those times when discipline comes our way. If we allow God to do His work in us over this thing that needs discipline, we will grow in our intimacy with Him. The training will yield the "peaceful fruit of righteousness." In other words, our walk will match our talk; the fruit of the training will be right behavior. We are already righteous in our spirits, in union with Christ—loving discipline from our heavenly Father makes that righteousness show up in our outward behavior. We do not have to be ashamed of discipline; it is good.

As I was thinking about an example I could use here, I was going over the verse in my mind and thinking about the part that talks about training, the other form of discipline—self-discipline. I realized that God trained me to walk by faith, so I began to look back at how He did that. He did it much the same way an athlete trains for a sport. Practice! Practice! Practice! He gave me lots and lots of opportunities to believe His word against the appearances and feelings that I could see and touch. Through relating to Him, He retrained my mind and emotions so that I saw life through His eyes.

All the years our family was in the ministry, not knowing how much money we would have each month slowly but surely taught me to trust God. Trials such as my divorce and later having to move out of my home brought emotional pain that were opportunities to turn to Jesus and cling to Him. Whenever I heard God's words in my spirit, such as the time when He told me to say I have a gentle and quiet spirit, (Devotion on I Peter 3:4 in the chapter on Grace and Union) I chose to obey Him, These are examples of trusting Him in spite of feelings and appearances.

Practice. Obedience. Faith. All are part of discipline. Like every good athlete, we have to follow all that our Coach has for us. I laugh inside when God reminds me that I have to do something that might feel embarrassing or I have to share a story about my failures. I laugh because, even though I might be hesitant, I do want to "walk what I talk" and "practice what I write and teach," and that helps me obey. Being humbled is one of the exercises that our Coach uses to teach us. It may not feel good to put aside our pride, but I'm grateful for both kinds of discipline that cause me to enjoy the peaceful fruit of righteousness.

Application: When you feel the sting of discipline—you have to humbly seek forgiveness from someone—you have to trust God to pay a bill, you have to confess a fault, or you have to say the truth about yourself—remember the reward is intimacy and the peaceful fruit of righteousness. Think on this quote from *Hinds' Feet on High Places:* "Love is beautiful, but it is also terrible—terrible in its determination to allow nothing blemished or unworthy to remain in the beloved."[94]

---

[94]Hannah Hurnard, *Hinds' Feet on High Places*, page 179.

"While we look not at the things which are seen, but at the things which are not seen; for the things which are seen are temporal, but the things which are not seen are eternal." II Corinthians 4:18

Just thinking about living as if an invisible world is more real than the visible one can make us feel a little crazy—until we experience what it's like to walk in intimacy with Christ in spite of feelings and circumstances. Looking at life through His perspective changes how we walk through life. When we know the differences in our soul and our spirit, we will walk with confidence that the spirit is fixed, un-moveable and sure. It will be easier to know the difference in God's voice and Satan's voice and easier to keep our focus on Jesus.

God's gentle voice is your comforting guide and He is always with you waiting to speak. He longs to break down all barriers that keep you from His love. He knows all about your past and present hurts that make your emotions swing; He longs to validate you, comfort you and heal you.

Application: Do you know what barriers you have erected to keep God at a distance? Let Him in. Take a risk. Borrow my faith, or someone else's faith that you trust, until you see that He is trustworthy, loving, kind, and safe. Finding intimacy with Him will result in peace, love, joy, and knowing who you are.

INTIMACY THROUGH PRAYER AND COMMUNION

"Be anxious for nothing, but in everything by prayer and supplication with thanksgiving, let your request be made known to God." Philippians, 4: 6

Paul is telling us here that we can pray about everything, especially when we're anxious. Unless you're a veteran prayer warrior, prayer might seem like a very mysterious and even frightening undertaking. Maybe you're accustomed to written, formal prayers. Perhaps you've never prayed. You're not sure how to pray and the last thing you want is to be called on to pray aloud. It's common to worry that we're not saying the right words or that the people listening to us pray will think our prayers are strange. Don't be anxious. Let's look at the different aspects of prayer and hopefully you will see how prayer will lead you to more intimacy with Christ.

Prayer is both simple and complex. Prayer is simple because it's just talking to God the same way we talk to each other. We don't have to say His name over and over or talk loudly and emotionally to get Him to hear us. He is ever-present and wants to communicate with us more than we can imagine. There are no special formulas, no exact patterns or sacred times. We can pray anytime, anywhere, because prayer can be done silently within our minds. We can pray with others, alone, aloud, or silently. Jesus wants to hear our concerns. He loves to hear our thanks and our requests. Supplication means we ask humbly.

On the other hand, prayer can seem complex, not only because we worry about how to do it correctly, but we worry that we won't get the answers for which we hope and desire. God answers every single prayer—He says either, "Yes," "No," or "Wait." Our problems arise when we don't get a quick, "Yes." We feel like we did not pray correctly—or that God doesn't care. When we don't get what we hoped for at the timing we wanted, we have to trust Him and walk by faith in His goodness—regardless of the answer. He is God. He knows best. He knows the whole picture.

Recently I had a short illness that made it hard to stand up or walk. It came on suddenly without warning and I wondered, "What if this happens again, out of the blue, while I'm driving? What if I have a grandchild in the car?" I started to feel anxious. I turned inside to Jesus, and knowing He does not want me to live by fear, I agreed with Him by saying, "I refuse to live by fear! I will not keep stirring this in my mind. You have not given me a spirit of fear." (Colossians 3:15; II Timothy 1:7; I John 4:18) I took a deep breath, did the chest-tapping exercise, and thanked Jesus that He is in control of all that comes into my life and all my loved ones as well. (Matthew 28:18) Now when the thoughts return, I refuse them again.

Application: Where are you on the topic of prayer? Do you feel comfortable talking to God silently? Are you able to pray aloud in front of others? What are you feeling anxious about these days? Talk to Jesus about anything and everything. Don't worry whether your words and form are correct. Just talk to Him like you do your best friend. If you know a "veteran prayer warrior," ask him or her to help you learn to pray aloud.

"Devote yourselves to prayer, keeping alert in it with an attitude of thanksgiving; praying at the same time for us as well, that God may open up to us a door for the word, so that we may speak forth the mystery of Christ for which I have also been imprisoned; in order that I may make it clear in the way I ought to speak." Colossians 4; 2-3

Paul wrote this verse to the people in Colossae when he was in prison. He asked them to pray "so that we may speak forth the mystery of Christ ... in order that I may make it clear in the way I ought to speak," for the sake of the Gospel. This aspect of prayer seems to call us to talk to Jesus when we sense we need to speak to someone about God or we see they have needs. We want to ask Jesus to open doors for speaking about Him to others and then let Him speak through us so that His words will be clear. Conversations and situations where we can talk about God with others can happen anytime, anyplace, in an instant; so we stay alert to His nudges. In that instant that we realize that someone needs a kind or comforting word, we can just ask Jesus to speak through us. We don't have to go to a special place to turn to Him. He is always right here in all of us who have received Him as Savior.

Everyone who knows Jesus can learn to "devote" themselves to prayer. Devote means to "set aside or give up oneself, time or energy." There are many teachings on what we sometimes call, "a quiet time." Special times with God are wonderful, healing and growing times. Years back when I first began to help other young women get to know God, I heard many of them lament that they could never find time to have a special time with God. Although that is a great way to spend time with God, I encouraged these young mothers to realize that their lives are like a prayer—that when they are washing dishes, doing laundry, changing diapers and carpooling, Jesus is living through them. They are praying. And—when at all possible, all during the day, they can talk to Him about everything that comes up.

> ***Application:*** It's great to have a special time and place to read the Bible and pray, but sometimes it can be very difficult. Do your best to find those times, but remember that Jesus does not want you to beat up on yourself because you miss a time or struggle to devote yourself. In some seasons of life, you can devote yourself by talking to Him all the time, everywhere.

"Pray without ceasing." 1 Thessalonians 5:17

This verse in Thessalonians intrigued me for years. I had a picture of myself something like a monk who seldom got off of his knees, except to eat, sleep or take care of bodily functions. There was no way that I could do that as a busy wife, mother and minister who had a house to take care of, friends to help, hobbies to enjoy and children to rear.

When I learned that Jesus was my life, always in me, wanting to live through me, I understood this verse for the first time—prayer became like breathing to me: I found myself talking to Jesus anytime, anywhere—as I enjoyed seeing something beautiful, praising Him in that beauty; when things weren't going well in the moment, asking Him about it; when someone was in need, asking Him to meet those needs. That's what it means to pray without ceasing. There is no separation of spiritual life and secular life.

Similar to what we saw in the last devotion, we do not have to sit down in a spot with our Bible and notebook in order to pray. It's fabulous when we can, but not necessary in order to connect with the God of the Universe who is our Father, Brother, Comforter, Healer, Provider, Lover, and everything else we need. He is Immanuel—God with us! He is always here.

Application: Do you remember to talk to Jesus off and on during your day? Do your best to have a special time, but purpose to form a habit of talking to Him all the time. Ask a friend or loved one to remind you to practice "praying without ceasing."

"Behold, the virgin shall be with child, and shall bear a Son and they shall call His name 'Immanuel,' which translated means, 'God with us.'" Matthew 1:23 (quoting Isaiah 7:14)

This verse that we often associate with Christmas can help us find an easy way to talk to Jesus that feels more like a conversation. In order to sense that we are "conversing" with Jesus, it helps to realize a few things first: As Christians, Jesus lives in us and wants to have a real relationship with us; we can learn to recognize His voice; we can believe that Jesus is not out to get us. [95] As we grow in knowledge of who He is and how much He loves us, hearing His voice will get easier and easier. Having a "conversation" with Him is what intimacy is all about!

A few months ago I had the opportunity to talk with Jesus about some insecure feelings I was experiencing when I was afraid that I had not done "a good enough job." I used a simple version of the "Immanuel Process" that I learned from Dr. Wilder.[96]

I like to use paper and pen when I sit down to talk to Jesus, but it's not necessary. It helps me keep my thoughts straight. I got out my journal and started writing my feelings about what was going on. Then I wrote as if talking to Jesus, asking Him, "What do you want me to know about these feelings I have that I might not have done a good enough job and thus embarrassed a friend? What made those feelings so big? What are they "triggering" from my past?"

As I sat quietly with Jesus, He brought to mind a memory of a time in high school when I was in a play and had stage fright while doing a short monologue. I was not devastated by this event, but since that's what He brought to mind, I looked at it and asked Him, "Where were You when that was going on?" He told me, *"I was behind the curtain smiling at your*

---

[95] See the devotion on Psalm 9:12 in the chapter on Faith and the devotions--I Corinthians 11:14 and I Kings 9: 11-12 in the chapter on Feelings and Appearances; and the chapter on Grace and Union.

[96] For more information on the Immanuel Process, see the *Share Immanuel* booklet at www.lifemodel.org, www.thrivetoday.org or articles on I. P. and triggering at www.kclehman.org

bravery to even try. It was not in your comfort zone. You handled it pretty well."

So I sat with Him for a few more minutes, sensing that was not the deepest issue, then I asked, "What do I need to know about why I feel such a need for my friend to say I did a good job?"

This time, Jesus reminded me of how many times I had done things both publicly and as ministry for others and received no appreciation or feedback. I remembered that this same topic had come up years ago when I was counseling with Dr. Wilder. At that time, Dr. Wilder told me that I believed it was bad or prideful to *want* appreciation and affirmation. He then explained that wanting those are not bad or prideful—it's a legitimate need that we all have. When that need is not met, it hurts. I accepted that truth and remembered it over the years, but since it was coming back up, I guessed Jesus wanted to take me further with it.

As I continued in His presence, this is part of what He said:

"'A workman is worthy of his hire.' I love you. You bring me joy all the time—just being you. I don't see your lacks—I see your heart and how you long for others to know this intimacy with Me and the Immanuel Process and all that you have learned. And even if your friend does say you were "off" or that you embarrassed him, that would not change who you are to Me or your value to Me.

Just look at Me and see how I love you. I was right there in all those things you listed from the past, smiling with delight at your courage or creativity—your heart that just wants to "teach" and help others. Know that I say, "You did a great job. You are you and I can use you as you are. I used a donkey and can even make rocks cry out if I need them to. Bloom where you are planted." (In my mind I saw Him smiling at me.)

Peace came to my soul as He spoke. I know He's our audience of one and we are to focus on Him, but isn't it wonderful how He wants us to share His love and show appreciation to one another—to even meet some of each others' needs? It feels so good to receive appreciation and so good to give it as well. Jesus validated and comforted my worry and healed some more wounds from the past.[97]

Application: When you have conflict where your emotions seem out of proportion to the circumstance, you may be "triggered" by something from your past which needs to be healed. Try talking to Jesus with some of these questions and listen for His voice, or see a counselor who can help. Jesus loves to comfort and heal so that you can be free from hurtful wounds.

"For this reason also, since the day we heard of it, we have not ceased to pray for you and to ask that you may be filled with the knowledge of His will in all spiritual wisdom and understanding, so that you may walk in a manner worthy of the Lord, to please Him in all respects, bearing fruit in every good work and increasing in the knowledge of God. . ." Colossians 1: 9-10

God has given us the wonderful privilege of praying for others as He stirs our hearts through His living, breathing presence in us. Through our ongoing conversations with God, the Holy Spirit quietly moves us, through our thoughts, to pray for someone. Likewise He moves others to pray for us. Unless we tell each other, these kinds of interactions are often unknown.

When someone I care about comes to my mind, I like to talk briefly to God about whatever is going on in their life. I use that time to just talk to God and pour out whatever I'm thinking without being too concerned what is or is not "His will." If my thoughts are along a line that I know is God's will from the Scriptures, such as praying for someone to come to salvation

---

[97] From my blog, *Audience of One* at www.barbaramoon.wordpress.com; For more information on the Immanuel Process, see the *Share Immanuel* booklet at www.lifemodel.org, www.thrivetoday.org or articles on Immanuel Process and triggering at www.kclehman.org

in Christ, then that makes the prayer easier. (In the next devotion we will look at what to do when we are not certain something is God's will.) Paul tells us here in Colossians to pray for others' growth and well being. Since we can know this kind of prayer is "God's will," we can believe that God will work to bring wisdom, understanding and good behavior to others' lives. Once I prayed this kind of prayer for a very important person in my life.

After a ten year gap in communication, my daughter, Jodi, reconnected with her teen-age friend, Rick, whom she had met at Space Camp in Huntsville, Alabama when she was 14 and Rick was 16. As they got re-acquainted, they began to talk about marriage. Through the years, since Jodi was a baby, I had prayed about who God would bring to her as her husband. I loved Rick and believed he was the kind of man for whom I'd been praying—except he was not a Christian.

When Rick asked me for Jodi's hand in marriage I told him I thought he was just the one for her, but it would be best if he loved God and wanted to follow Him. As we talked, Rick shared that he had questions because he wanted to know what he was getting into. When I heard that statement from his heart, I felt in my spirit that he would receive Jesus. Sure enough, a few weeks later Rick told us he had asked Jesus into his heart. My joy was full.

Now that Rick was a believer, it was easy to sense God prompting me to pray that Rick would have all those things that Paul prayed for the Colossians in this verse. The answer to that prayer came a year or so later when Rick was chosen to be mentored by a godly man at our church. Along with other men, they met weekly for a year. Rick grew in wisdom, knowledge, and understanding of God and the Scriptures. He grew in his walk with Jesus, pleasing Him as a father, husband, friend, and worker. I see the fruit that Rick bears in his love for his wife and his two sons, the work he does to help others know Jesus, and the kindness that flows from his heart. Rick is a great answer to prayer.

Application: Think of someone in your life who needs to be filled with the knowledge of God. Pray this verse aloud inserting their name.

Lift them up to God. Thank God for the people who have prayed, or are praying, for you that you may not even know about.

". . . and pray for one another so that you may be healed. The effective prayer of a righteous man can accomplish much." James 5:16b

James tells us here that prayers are "effective" when prayed by a "righteous man." Righteous men and women are people who know Jesus and are in tune with Him. The Spirit prompts and prays through us when we listen and co-operate. It's not our words that make things happen; it's that we are in tune with God's leading. It's as if God is praying through us, back to Himself about whatever He leads us to pray. When the promptings are clearly Scriptural, such as salvation and growth in the knowledge of God, we can pray with certainty that it's God's will. If what we're praying concerns another person, that person will also have to co-operate with God, but that part is not our problem—our call is to pray.

When we are not certain from the Scriptures that something is "God's will," it's easy to struggle with the prayer. Whenever possible, it helps to see if we *can know* what His will is in the situation. Sometimes we will get a sense of what He wants us to pray. Sometimes we just don't know for sure, but we can tell Him what we hope for and want. Part of growing in intimacy with Christ is this process of praying to find His will before praying; part of intimacy is trusting Him when we don't know or when we don't get what we wanted and hoped for. Physical healing, as James talks about here, is one of those issues. God can heal anything, but healing on Earth does not always happen. Our call, as "righteous men and women," is to talk to Him about everything and trust Him no matter what the outcome. As we get to know God's voice better and better, we will grow in our experiences of effective prayer.

Application: Are you learning to know God's voice and listen when He prompts you to pray? He so longs to be intimate with you and show you His love even when things do not work out as you planned. Take time to *find* His will when you're not sure how to pray. If you're not sure, trust His love and know that He always knows the whole picture and what's best.

"We give thanks to God, the Father of our Lord Jesus Christ, praying always for you." Colossians 1:2

Our intimacy with Christ grows as we learn how to pray. In the devotion for I Thessalonians 5:17 we talked about one form of prayer that was "without ceasing." We considered that this form of prayer was almost like breathing—talking to God throughout the day about whatever comes up. Now let's look at a more structured form of prayer in which we sit down in a quiet place with our Bible and some kind of journal or notebook in which to keep track of our concerns and prayers.

My first prayer journal was a notebook broken down into sections designed to help a person write down what they wanted to pray about in different categories such as, family, government, church, career, and finances.[98] The sections helped me think about who I could be praying about as I talked to Jesus. When I learned how to write down my concerns and pray specifically for people instead of just saying, "Bless _____, Lord." I began to realize that God did answer because I could look back at what I had written down and see how and when God answered the request.

---

[98] Notebook from Peter Lord, a pastor from Titusville, Florida, whom I have mentioned before. The notebook's title was *2959* which stood for "29 minutes and 59 seconds." The idea was to try to get to the point that one could spend at least 30 minutes with God.

For me, and for many others, using a journal to write down what I've mentioned to God has helped me remember, and then celebrate, when I see His answers to my prayers. Having a written record of answers has helped me grow in confidence that He hears me, and has encouraged more intimacy with Him.[99]

While there are many great prayer plans out there that you can purchase to help you get started, one easy one I would like to share with you is the acronym ACTS.[100] You can use the ACTS acronym as a guide whether you write down your prayers or speak them.

Adoration: saying what's true and good about God back to him.

Example: "Father, You are merciful and full of grace. You are kind and loving. You love us just as we are while You see what You can do to help us grow."

Confession: checking to see if there is anything we are not obeying or that we are doing that needs changing and then asking God's forgiveness.

Example: "Father, I confess that right now I don't feel much like praying. I am upset with _____. There are problems at work and people that are hard to get along with. I know my attitude is not good. I ask You to forgive me and show me how You want to work in these situations."

Thanksgiving: showing gratitude for what God has done and continues to do for us and the world.

Example: "Father, I thank You for Your grace and mercy and Your provision. I thank You for my health and the health of my family. I thank You that we have food and shelter. I thank You, Jesus, for dying on the Cross for us."

---

[99] There are many places to purchase journals in which to write down your prayers to God.

[100] I first heard about ACTS as a way to pray back in the 70's. I never knew who came up with it, but when checking online I found a book by E. W. Price, Jr.; *ACTS in Prayer*; B&H Publishing Group, 1974. Since this book is so old, I assume it is the origin.

Supplication: ask God for what we need, what we want Him to do for us and others.

Example: "Father, I lift up my friend _____ to You. She is hurting right now because of her divorce. I ask You to comfort her and show her the way through. I ask You to keep my children/family safe today. I pray for our pastor and his family that You will protect them from the enemy who wants to destroy their good name and ministry. I pray for our government leaders and for my children's teachers. In Jesus' name I pray. Amen."

Application: In this more structured form of prayer, be as specific as you can when you pray. Find a place to write down what you want God to do, who you are talking to Him about, and your concerns. Then you will be more likely to notice the answers. Now and then, go back over what you have talked about to God and write down the answers, thanking Him for His faithfulness and care.

"And when He arrived at the place, He said to them, 'Pray that you may not enter into temptation.'" Luke 22: 40

"... the spirit is willing, but the flesh is weak." Mark 14: 38b

Jesus gives us another reason to pray here in Luke. He took the disciples to the mountain and moved away to pray. He asked them to pray so that they would not enter into temptation. They fell asleep instead of praying. We are so like the disciples. "The spirit is willing but the flesh is weak." The intent of our heart is to serve, follow, love, and obey God at all times, but it's so easy to "fall asleep." We forget that Jesus is, and always was, and always will be with us. We forget to turn to Him in a moment of conflict or trial. I remember one time when I was in elementary school and a friend wanted me to steal something. We were at a little variety store. I knew better, but I joined her and took a pair of mittens. I was very bothered by this and never told anyone. I did ask Jesus to forgive me, but that awful guilty feeling was a good deterrent from stealing again.

There was another time in high school where I didn't know the answer to a test question. I could feel that pull to just take the risk for a quick look at a neighbor's paper. I could also hear Jesus telling me in my mind that I better not do it. I resisted the pull to cheat and wrote down the best answer I knew.

While growing up I was the kind of person who *mostly* did the right thing. I had a bent towards following rules and being "a good little girl." Sometimes when most of our actions look right, God has a difficult time showing us things He needs to change because the changes needed are more in our thoughts and attitudes. When other people don't see what's going on inside of us, it's easy to be prideful and ignore God's conviction. But it's important to turn to Him with those negative thoughts and bad attitudes as well. Since we are "in Him," we do not have to resist temptations in our own strength. We have His power within us and all we have to do is pray—talk to Him.

Application: Is there a place that you experience recurring temptation? Agree with God that you cannot fight this on your own. You may need to find someone like a trusted friend or a professional to help as you learn to talk to Him and tap in to His power. "Therefore, confess your sins to one another and pray for one another so that you may be healed." James 5: 16a

"Is anyone among you sick? Let him call for the elders of the church, and let them pray for him, anointing him with oil in the name of the Lord." James 5:14

"Concerning this *(thorn in the flesh)* **I entreated the Lord three times that it might depart from me. And He said to me, 'My grace is sufficient for you, for power is perfected in weakness.' Most gladly therefore I will rather boast about my weaknesses that the power of Christ may dwell in me." II Corinthians 12: 8-9** *(parentheses mine)*

Praying for physical healing is a much debated issue. Some people believe that all illnesses should be healed; others do not. I certainly do not know the answer to "why some people are not physically healed," but I *do* know the Lord who comforts those who are ill or left behind. James tells us here that we can pray for healing; we see the healing is up to God. Paul asked God three times to take away his "thorn in the flesh," but God told Paul that His grace was sufficient to bear it and that Paul would see God's power in his weakness. Not being healed physically is very difficult to bear and/or watch. The only way to get through the difficulty is to turn to Jesus and hold on to Him.

When our third son, Greg, was born he did not thrive. I took him time after time to the small-town doctor in Kentucky where we lived. Finally through the kindness of a friend, I found a doctor in the next town who realized that Greg had a serious heart condition. We rushed him to the University of Kentucky Medical Center and left him overnight for tests. The next morning the doctors there told us that he most likely would not live more than a couple of years. We were devastated. We took him back home with some experimental medicine. This was the first real trial that had come into my life.

Two weeks later Greg had to return to a hospital in the next little town and I stayed with him. I walked to the town library to check out some books to read. I found one that talked about turning to God when circumstances were difficult and painful. I remember telling God something like this: "This is Your baby. I give Him back to You for You to do with what You want to do." Most likely, I did this with much innocence, but it was sincere. For the next eight years, we did not know if Greg would grow up or not. When he was eight, the doctor told us that his heart was a normal size and we did not have to return for check-ups. I don't believe that God healed Greg because I "surrendered" to His will. I believe God healed Greg because He had a purpose for Greg's life. Today he, his wonderful wife, and their four daughters love and serve God.

I can't say what I would be like today if God had not healed Greg, but I like to believe that I would have kept learning to turn to Him. I've had other painful events that have shaped my walk in intimacy, many that didn't turn out like I'd hoped, but this I can tell you—if you or a loved one needs a physical healing, whether God says, "Yes" or He says, "No," you will find Him true to His word that He is with you and He is love. (I John 4:8) His grace will be sufficient.

> ***Application:*** Are you or someone you love facing physical illness? Talk to Jesus and ask to sense His comforting presence regardless of the outcome. No matter what happens, He loves you, He is with you, and He understands. He feels the hurt with you.

"The cup of blessing which we bless, is it not the communion of the blood of Christ? The bread which we break, is it not the communion of the body of Christ?" I Corinthians 10: 16 KJV

"The grace of the Lord Jesus Christ, and the love of God, and the communion of the Holy Ghost, be with you all. Amen." II Corinthians 13: 14

These two verses show us how prayer and communion, ("the Lord's Supper") go together. In both verses the same Greek word is used for the ordinance of "communion" with the cup and the bread and "communion," or prayer with the Holy Spirit. The Greek word is *kononia* which is also translated as "fellowship."

In the Greek language, the word fellowship gives us a picture of intimacy—"two fellows sharing the same ship." For me the emphasis here is on the words *sharing* and *same*. In fellowship, whether the other person is God with whom we are sharing prayer, is blood kin (family), or is a friend, the deepest communion comes only when the two (or more) share God's values and God's ways.

The word *kononia* also has the connotation of "intercourse," another of its meaning in the Greek. Intercourse here does not mean sex, it means true intimacy—an authentic relationship based on sharing the same way God shares. True intimacy is knowing and being known, loving and being loved—a safe ship for experiencing innermost openness. Safe openness is what we want, and can have, with Jesus.

One day as I was thinking about fellowship and communion in regards to true intimacy, it occurred to me that I could see "common union" in the word. Common union is the idea I am trying to get to here about intimacy in prayer. It's something deeper than friendship and kinship, though we certainly can have common union with both friends and kin. When we connect with God in prayer and hear His voice back and forth, there is nothing like it.[101] God designed us to live that way, filled with joy and with an authentic, deep, intimate, connected relationship.[102]

Application: Are you experiencing true fellowship and openness with God? Are you learning that He is a "safe ship" and that you can trust Him? Do you have other people with whom you can be open and vulnerable and with whom you feel safe to share the same ship? If not, seek help so that you may enjoy common union.

---

[101] See devotion II Corinthians 11:14 on the "Two Voices," Chapter on Barriers to Intimacy.

[102] Taken from my blog, *Friendship, Fellowship, Kinship,* www.barbaramoon.wordpress.com

"**And when He had taken some bread and given thanks, He broke it, and gave it to them, saying, 'This is my body which is given for you. Do this in remembrance of Me.' And in the same way He took the cup after they had eaten saying, 'This cup poured out for you is the new covenant in My blood.'" Luke 22; 19-20**

Usually when we think of the word communion, rather than thinking about fellowship, we think about what some call the "Lord's Supper." Let's put the two concepts together and see if it will move us further down the path to intimacy. The cup is for the juice/wine that represents Jesus' blood. The bread represents His body. Two elements—two symbols. These two symbols show us there are two sides to the Cross. The verse we have here is often read during Communion. I had it memorized, but I didn't realize that there's a reason there are two elements—the cup and the bread.

I learned the following thoughts from Dan Stone and they blessed me greatly. I had never heard anyone speak about Communion as Dan did, and his viewpoint is a kind of summary of all we have looked at in several chapters.[103]

The first side of the Cross is the blood side. That's where *Christ died for* our sins—"sins" plural. The blood was for God. Because of Adam and Eve's sin in the Garden of Eden, someone had to pay the price for mankind to be restored to a relationship with God. By God's design, that price was blood.[104] Jesus paid the price with His blood so

---

[103] From *The Rest of the Gospel,* pages 39-43.

[104] We looked at the blood sacrifice in the chapter on Salvation, devotion Colossians 1:13-14. Hebrews 9:22(NLT): "In fact, according to the law of Moses,

we can be forgiven. After receiving Christ as our personal Savior, our sins are forgiven—past-present-and future. But there is another side to the Cross.

The second side of the Cross is the body side. That's where *we died with* Christ.[105] The body side is for us—we had to die so that the power of sin— "sin" singular—would be broken in our lives We were united with Him on the Cross, participating in His death, burial, and resurrection. Our old man was crucified with Him. Our new man— righteous and holy—was resurrected with Him.

Most people I (Dan) have known have not experienced freedom from sin so they concluded they would only live in victory after they died and went to Heaven. But God's promises are meant to be experienced now. Yes, we have to die, but the question is, "When did we die?"[106]

These two sides of the Cross are not unfamiliar to us. We celebrate them every time we take Communion. We eat the bread. We drink the cup. Most of us realize what the cup and blood are representing, but do we know what the bread represents? The bread represents His body, and because we have been baptized into Christ, we were in that body with Him—what happened to Him happened to us. [107]

Another word for baptize is "to immerse, or place into." When we make our coffee we immerse sugar and cream into the coffee and they become one. The sugar and cream go wherever the coffee goes. If wool is dyed, the colors permeate the wool. In the same way, we were united with Him, and when He died, we died. When He was buried, we were buried. When He was raised, we were raised. The heart of Paul's

---

nearly everything was purified with blood. For without the shedding of blood, there is no forgiveness."

[105] We looked at our death with Christ in the Chapter on Grace and Union, devotions Romans 6:6 and Galatians 2:20

[106] We saw clearly in the Chapter on Grace and Union that we died with Christ.

[107]Galatians 3:27: "For all of you who were baptized into Christ have clothed yourselves with Christ.

message is built on the Lord's Supper: the blood and the body. Christ died *for* us: we died *with* Him.

In the unseen and eternal realm, "above the line," an exchange has taken place in our spirit that, once we know it, produces through us a quality of life that's different from anything else the world has seen. It's light in darkness. It's other-love in a world of self-love. It's desirable. And it's in us

We don't feel dead. We don't look dead. We often don't act dead. But at some point the Holy Spirit pulls back the curtain and shows us that in the deepest part of us, our spirit—who we truly are—a death and a resurrection have occurred that has forever changed us. We're going to look the same, feel the same, and think the same on many, many days. But after the Holy Spirit pulls back the curtain, we're going to know something: we are not the same.[108]

> ***Application:*** Can you see the intimacy here with the One who died to forgive you and set you free? We cannot get any closer to Jesus than to be one with Him: baptized into His death and raised with Him to a new life. The next time you take Communion, think about the two sides to the Cross—the blood is for God and the body is for you. Rejoice afresh that you died with Christ.

"That they may all be one; even as Thou Father are in Me and I in Thee, that they also may be in Us, that the world may believe that Thou didst send Me. And the glory which Thou has given

---

[108] Paraphrased from *The Rest of the Gospel*, Pages 39-43

Me, I have given to them, so that they may be one, just as We are one. . ." John 17: 21-22

As we near the end of our chapter about intimacy through prayer and communion, I would like to share some examples from my own life. While learning how to talk to God and listen for His voice in prayer, I've found it very helpful to interact with Him through journaling my thoughts and feelings, and then asking Him to give me His take on it. Writing down my prayers and struggles is like a diary to God. Journaling keeps my mind on what I'm praying about, with an added plus that I feel like I've left the problems there in my journal, as if they are in God's lap.

After I've written out my prayers and current struggles, through the *Immanuel Process*, I've learned to ask Jesus, "What do you want me to know about that?"[109] Then I write down what I sense that He is saying back to me in my mind and heart. I trust that what I am sensing is Him, because I've asked Him, "What do You want me to know?" Sometimes I just ask Him, "What do You want to say to me tonight?" He might want to heal something painful and/or say some loving words to me. Either way, I'm enjoying some lovely conversations with Jesus.

Perhaps you're wondering what it means to have a "conversation" with Jesus. Remember the devotion in the chapter on Faith, Psalm 91:2 where we looked at getting to know God the same way people who drive their cars out onto a frozen lake "know the ice?" Remember the devotion from II Corinthians 11:14 in the chapter on Barriers to Intimacy about the "Two Voices?" Refresh yourself on these two devotions as you look at my examples here and consider the possibility that you can have a "conversation" with Jesus. Knowing Jesus is a relationship like any other. That's what intimacy is all about. He longs for us to know and interact with Him on a deep level. He is patient to teach us and guide us in that direction. As we get to know His voice, it becomes easier to recognize that He wants to interact intimately, back and forth with us.

One Sunday night, before I went to bed, I was journaling about the day—especially about the sweet worship I had experienced at church that

---

[109]*Share Immanuel* booklet by Dr. Wilder and Chris Coursey, available at www.lifemodel.org and www.thrivetoday.org

morning, and then about a circumstance that was causing me some pain. Here is what I heard from Him after asking Him what He wanted me to know:

> *"You are My delight. I saw you loving on Me at church. I like that song, too. I like you even more.* (I saw Him smiling.)
>
> *I'm proud of you today for coming to me when that knot came in your stomach. You listen to me. I will make things clear anytime. You are not making this up.* (A smile again).
>
> *I want you to help others with the Immanuel Process. Some will listen and learn. I just love you so much, My Daughter. You bring Me joy all the time. I want you to know ever more deeply how awesome you are. I will complete the work I have begun. If you need it (or want it), I will affirm you and brag on you any time."* (Another smile).

[I would love that, Lord.]

> *"I see you through Heaven's eyes."* (Now chuckling)

[I love You, Jesus]

Another time, I felt burdened to pray for family and friends who were really struggling with circumstances in their own lives. After I wrote down their names, I asked Jesus, "What do You want me to know tonight?" and here is what I heard from Him:

> *"I love you, Precious. Enjoy Connor and Ryan tomorrow. They bring you joy. I am taking care of the people you named. Just rest in My lap. My love and My life will flow through you to many. Enjoy the group you are teaching again."*

[Thank You, Lord][110]

Application: If having a back and forth conversation with Jesus is new to you, I encourage you to give it a try. Keep in mind that you are

---

[110] Taken from my blog, *Conversations With Jesus,*
www.barbaramoon.wordpress.com

"one with Him." (I Corinthians 6:17) After you have told Him about a situation and/or how you are feeling, ask "What do you want me to know about this?" Sit quietly and trust that what you hear is from Him unless it is not like His character. The words you will hear will be validating, comforting, loving, encouraging—and even fun. He has a sense of humor—He invented laughter. His words are designed for you to know He is with you no matter what is going on. It's best to stay away from "why" questions, because He doesn't often answer those kinds of questions.[111] He sees the big picture—He wants us to walk by faith and trust Him no matter what.

"Be anxious for nothing, but in everything by prayer and supplication with thanksgiving, let your request be made known to God." Philippians, 4: 6

"With all prayer and petition pray at all times in the Spirit, and with this in view, be on the alert with all perseverance and petition for all the saints." Ephesians 6:18 (New Living Translation)

Prayer is simply talking to God the same as we talk to others. We don't have to fear that we're not using the right words or not praying correctly. We talk to God in our own way, anytime, anywhere. We have "common union" with Him, both when praying and taking the "Lord's Supper." Common union is possible because of Jesus' death and resurrection and that He now lives in us. During Communion, we remember what He has done to take care of all our sins by His blood, and

---

[111] *Share Immanuel* booklet, page 9; also more information on Immanuel Process at www.kclehman.com

that we have a completely new life through our death with His body. The door to intimacy is wide open; all we have to do is talk to Jesus and trust Him to know what's best. We can pray "at all times," anywhere.

Application: When you feel anxious, turn to Jesus and talk to Him about whatever is going on, and wait to hear His voice in return.[112] He wants you to feel safe, comforted, and encouraged. Practice trusting that what you hear in your mind and heart is Him speaking to you. You *can* get to know His voice. Intimacy *will* grow as you practice interacting with Jesus through prayer.

---

[112] See devotion II Corinthians 11:14 on the "Two Voices," Chapter on Barriers to Intimacy

RECOMMENDED READING

The Rest of the Gospel: When the partial Gospel has worn you out, Dan Stone

Hinds' Feet on High Places, Hannah Hurnard

Lifetime Guarantee, Bill Gillham

The Confident Woman, Anabel Gillham

Handbook to Happiness, Dr. Charles Solomon

Turkeys and Eagles, Peter Lord

Birthright: Christian Do You Know Who You Are? David Needham

Jesus Never Fails: Stories of God's Faithfulness, Barbara Moon

Joy-Filled Relationships, Barbara Moon

Handbook to Joy-Filled Parenting, Barbara Moon

The Life Model, Living from the Heart Jesus Gave You, www.lifemodel.org

Joy Starts Here, Wilder, Khouri, Coursey, Sutton, www.lifemodel.org

RESOURCES

www.lifemodel.org

www.thrivetoday.org

www.kclehman.com

www.lifetime.org

Made in the USA
Lexington, KY
10 July 2013